Why Pray?

Selected from
*Prayer: What Difference
Does It Make?*

Why Pray?

Philip Yancey

rbc
ministries

∼ Contents

~ Why Pray?

∽ Our Deepest Longing

When a doctoral student at Princeton asked, "What is there left in the world for original dissertation research?" Albert Einstein replied, "Find out about prayer. Somebody must find out about prayer."

I CHOSE THE WRONG TIME to visit St. Petersburg, Russia. I went in November of 2002 just as the city was reconstructing itself to prepare for its three hundredth birthday the following year. Scaffolding covered every building of note and rubble littered the quaint cobblestone streets, which turned my morning jogging routine into an adventure. I ran in darkness (the sun rose mid-morning at that latitude) with my head down, dodging the workmen's piles of brick and sand while glancing ahead for the dim gloss that betrayed the presence of ice.

I must have lost concentration one morning, for suddenly I found myself facedown on the street, dazed and shivering. I sat up. I could remember jerking my head sideways as I fell, to avoid a piece of steel rebar protruding from the curb at a wicked angle. I removed my gloves, reached for my right eye, and felt blood. The entire right side of my face was wet with blood. I got up, dusted dirt and flecks of snow from my running suit, and felt for more damage. I walked slowly, testing my throbbing knees and elbows. I tasted blood, and a couple of blocks away I realized a front tooth was missing. I returned to search for it in the dark, in vain.

WHY PRAY?

When I reached Nevsky Prospekt, a busy boulevard, I noticed that people were staring at me. Russians rarely look strangers in the eye, so I must have been a sight. I limped to the hotel and talked my way past dubious security guards to get to my room. I knocked on the door and said, "Janet, let me in—I'm hurt."

We had both heard horror stories about medical care in Russia, where you can go in with a surface wound and come out with AIDS or hepatitis. I decided on self-treatment. After raiding the minibar for tiny bottles of vodka, we started cleaning the scrapes on my face. My upper lip was split in two. I gritted my teeth, poured the alcohol over the cuts, and scrubbed my face with a packaged refresher-cloth left over from the Lufthansa flight. We taped the lip together tightly with a Band-Aid, hoping it would heal straight. By now the area around my eye had swollen and turned a spectacular purple, but fortunately my sight seemed unimpaired.

I took a few aspirin and rested awhile. Then I went back out to Nevsky Prospekt and looked for an Internet café. I climbed three flights of stairs, used sign language to negotiate the price in rubles, and settled in at a computer terminal. My fingers rested on a strange keyboard and I faced the Cyrillic alphabet onscreen. After ten minutes of false starts, I finally found my way to an AOL screen in English. Ah, connected at last. I typed a note to a prayer group at my home church in Colorado and to a few friends and family members. The wireless network kept cutting on and off, and each time I had to find AOL again and retype the message.

The message was simple: a few background details, then "We need help. Please pray." I didn't know the extent of my injuries. The next few days I was supposed to speak at a booksellers' convention in St. Petersburg, then go on to Moscow for more speaking assignments. The news banner on AOL was telling me that armed Chechen rebels had just seized a theater full of patrons and Moscow was under military lockdown. I finished my message and pressed "Send" just as a warning popped up informing me my time was running out.

Is this how prayer works? I wondered as I walked back to the hotel. We send signals from a visible world to an invisible one, in hope that Someone receives them. And how will we know?

Still, for the first time that day I felt the lump of fear and anxiety in my stomach begin to loosen. In a few hours my friends and family, people who cared, would turn on their computers, read my message, and pray on my behalf. I was not alone.*

A Universal Cry

Every faith has some form of prayer. Remote tribes present offerings and then pray for everyday things such as health, food, rain, children, and victory in battles. Incas and Aztecs went so far as to sacrifice humans in order to attract the gods' attention. Five times a day modern Muslims stop whatever they are doing—driving, having a coffee break, playing soccer—when the summons comes to pray.

Even atheists find ways to pray. During the heady days of Communism in Russia, true believers kept a "red corner," placing a portrait of Lenin where Christians used to keep their icons. Caught up in the fervor, *Pravda* ran this advice to its readers in 1950:

> If you meet with difficulties in your work, or suddenly doubt your abilities, think of him—of Stalin—and you will find the confidence you need. If you feel tired in an hour when you should not, think of him—of Stalin—and your work will go well. If you are seeking a correct decision, think of him—of Stalin—and you will find that decision.†

We pray because we want to thank someone or something for the beauties and glories of life, and also because we feel small and helpless and sometimes afraid. We pray for forgiveness, for strength, for contact

---

* Everything healed fine. And the request for prayer had one very practical benefit. The wife of my dentist, who was on the prayer team and received the message, immediately reserved an appointment for me so that the day after my return from Russia I had a root canal procedure!

† Quotations from other sources, including the Bible, are referenced at the back of the book.

with the One who is, for assurance that we are not alone. Millions in AA groups pray daily to a Higher Power, begging for help in controlling their addictions. We pray because we can't help it. The very word *prayer* comes from the Latin root *precarius*—a linguistic cousin to *precarious*. In St. Petersburg, Russia, I prayed out of desperation. I had nowhere else to turn.

Prayer is universal because it speaks to some basic human need. As Thomas Merton put it, "Prayer is an expression of who we are. . . . We are a living incompleteness. We are a gap, an emptiness that calls for fulfillment." In prayer we break silence, and sometimes those words flow out of our deepest parts. I remember in the days after September 11, 2001, saying over and over the prayer, "God, bless America." "Save America" is what I meant. Save us. Let us live. Give us another chance.

According to Gallup polls, more Americans will pray this week than will exercise, drive a car, have sex, or go to work. Nine in ten of us pray regularly, and three out of four claim to pray every day. To get some idea of the interest in prayer, type "prayer" or "pray" in an Internet search engine like Google and see how many millions of links pop up. Yet behind those impressive numbers lies a mystery.

When I started exploring the subject of Christian prayer, I first went to libraries and read accounts of some of the great pray-ers in history. George Müller began each day with several hours of prayer, imploring God to meet the practical needs of his orphanage. Bishop Lancelot Andrewes allotted five hours per day to prayer and Charles Simeon rose at 4:00 a.m. to begin his four-hour regimen. An order of nuns known as "The Sleepless Ones" still pray in shifts through every hour of the day and night. Susannah Wesley, a busy mother with no privacy, would sit in a rocking chair with an apron over her head praying for John and Charles and the rest of her brood. Martin Luther, who devoted two to three hours daily to prayer, said we should do it as naturally as a shoemaker makes a shoe and a tailor makes a coat. Jonathan Edwards wrote of the "sweet hours" on the banks of the Hudson River, "rapt and swallowed up in God."

In the next step I interviewed ordinary people about prayer. Typically, the results went like this: Is prayer important to you? *Oh, yes.* How often do you pray? *Every day.* Approximately how long? *Five minutes—well, maybe seven.* Do you find prayer satisfying? *Not really.* Do you sense the presence of God when you pray? *Occasionally, not often.* Many of those I talked to experienced prayer more as a burden than as a pleasure. They regarded it as important, even paramount, and felt guilty about their failure, blaming themselves.

A Modern Struggle

When I listened to public prayers in evangelical churches, I heard people telling God what to do, combined with thinly veiled hints on how others should behave. When I listened to prayers in more liberal churches, I heard calls to action, as if prayer were something to get past so we can do the real work of God's kingdom. Hans Küng's theological tome *On Being A Christian*, 702 pages long, did not include a chapter or even an index entry on prayer. When asked later, Küng said he regretted the oversight. He was feeling so harassed by Vatican censors and by his publisher's deadlines that he simply forgot about prayer.

Why does prayer rank so high on surveys of theoretical importance and so low on surveys of actual satisfaction? What accounts for the disparity between Luther and Simeon on their knees for several hours and the modern pray-er fidgeting in a chair after ten minutes?

Everywhere, I encountered the gap between prayer in theory and prayer in practice. In theory prayer is the essential human act, a priceless point of contact with the God of the universe. In practice prayer is often confusing and fraught with frustration. My publisher conducted a website poll, and of the 678 respondents only 23 felt satisfied with the time they were spending in prayer. That very discrepancy made me want to write this book.

Advances in science and technology no doubt contribute to our confusion about prayer. In former days farmers lifted their heads and appealed to brazen heavens for an end to drought. Now we study low-pressure fronts, dig irrigation canals, and seed clouds with metallic particles. In former days when a child fell ill the parents cried out to God; now they call for an ambulance or phone the doctor.

In much of the world, modern skepticism taints prayer. We breathe in an atmosphere of doubt. Why does God let history lurch on without intervening? What good will prayer do against a nuclear threat, against terrorism and hurricanes and global climate change? To some people prayer seems, as George Buttrick put it, "a spasm of words lost in a cosmic indifference"—and he wrote those words in 1942.

Prosperity may dilute prayer too. In my travels I have noticed that Christians in developing countries spend less time pondering the effectiveness of prayer and more time actually praying. The wealthy rely on talent and resources to solve immediate problems, and insurance policies and retirement plans to secure the future. We can hardly pray with sincerity, "Give us this day our daily bread" when the pantry is stocked with a month's supply of provisions.

Increasingly, time pressures crowd out the leisurely pace that prayer seems to require. Communication with other people keeps getting shorter and more cryptic: text messages, email, instant messaging. We have less and less time for conversation, let alone contemplation. We have the constant sensation of *not enough*: not enough time, not enough rest, not enough exercise, not enough leisure. Where does God fit into a life that already seems behind schedule?

If we do choose to look inward and bare our souls, therapists and support groups now offer outlets that were once reserved for God alone. Praying to an invisible God does not bring forth the same feedback you would get from a counselor or from friends who at least nod their heads in sympathy. Is anyone really listening? As Ernestine, the nasal-voiced telephone operator played by comedian Lily Tomlin, used to ask, "Have I reached the party to whom I am speaking?"

Prayer is to the skeptic a delusion, a waste of time. To the believer it represents perhaps the most important use of time. As a Christian, I believe the latter. Why, then, must prayer be so problematic? The British pastor Martyn Lloyd-Jones summed up the confusion: "Of all the activities in which the Christian engages, and which are part of the Christian life, there is surely none which causes so much perplexity, and raises so many problems, as the activity which we call prayer."

Pilgrim Quest

I write about prayer as a pilgrim, not an expert. I have the same questions that occur to almost everyone at some point. Is God listening? Why should God care about me? If God knows everything, what's the point of prayer? Why do answers to prayer seem so inconsistent, even capricious? Does a person with many praying friends stand a better chance of physical healing than one who also has cancer but with only a few people praying for her? Why does God sometimes seem close and sometimes far away? Does prayer change God or change me?

Before beginning this book I mostly avoided the topic of prayer out of guilt and a sense of inferiority. I'm embarrassed to admit that I do not keep a journal, do not see a spiritual director, and do not belong to a regular prayer group. And I readily confess that I tend to view prayer through a skeptic's lens, obsessing more about unanswered prayers than rejoicing over answered ones. In short, my main qualification for writing about prayer is that I feel unqualified—and genuinely want to learn.

More than anything else in life, I want to know God. The psychiatrist Gerald C. May observed, "After twenty years of listening to the yearnings of people's hearts, I am convinced that human beings have an inborn desire for God. Whether we are consciously religious or not, this desire is our deepest longing and most precious treasure." Surely, if we are made in God's own image, God will find a way of responding to that deepest longing. Prayer is that way.

By journalistic instinct, I asked many other people about prayer: my neighbors, other authors, fellow church members, spiritual mentors, ordinary people. I have included some of their reflections in drop-in boxes scattered throughout the book, as examples of actual down-to-earth encounters with prayer and also as a reminder to myself not to stray far from their questions. I use mostly first names, though some of them are well-known in Christian circles, to avoid any kind of hierarchy. When it comes to prayer we are all beginners.

I have not attempted a guidebook that details techniques such as fasting, prayer retreats, and spiritual direction. I investigate the topic of prayer as a pilgrim, strolling about, staring at the monuments, asking questions, mulling things over, testing the waters. I admit to an imbalance, an overreaction to time spent among Christians who promised too much and pondered too little, and as a result I try to err on the side of honesty and not pretense.

In the process of writing, however, I have come to see prayer as a privilege, not a duty. Like all good things, prayer requires some discipline. Yet I believe that life with God should seem more like friendship than duty. Prayer includes moments of ecstasy and also dullness, mindless distraction and acute concentration, flashes of joy and bouts of irritation. In other words, prayer has features in common with all relationships that matter.

If prayer stands as the place where God and human beings meet, then I must learn about prayer. Most of my struggles in the Christian life circle around the same two themes: why God doesn't act the way we want God to, and why I don't act the way God wants me to. Prayer is the precise point where those themes converge.

∿ View from Above

We must stop setting our sights by the light of each passing ship; instead we must set our course by the stars.

—GEORGE MARSHALL

To CLIMB A 14,000-FOOT mountain in Colorado you need an early start—as in four o'clock in the morning early—but you need to limit coffee intake in order to avoid dehydration. You drive on chassis-slapping rutted roads in the dark, always alert for wildlife, gaining elevation to somewhere between 9,000 and 10,000 feet, where the hiking trail begins. Then you begin the hike by wending your way through a forest of blue spruce, lodgepole pine, and Douglas fir on a trail that feels spongy underfoot from fallen needles. The ground gives off a pungent smell of decay and earth. You walk beside a tumbling creek, silvery white in the predawn moonlight, its burbling the only sound until the birds awake.

Around 11,000 feet the trees thin, giving way to lush meadows carpeted in wildflowers. The sun is rising now, first casting a reddish alpenglow on the mountaintops, then dropping its rays into the basins. Bright clumps of lupine, fireweed, columbine, and Indian paintbrush dapple the open spaces, while plants with more exotic names—monk's hood, elephant head, bishop's cap, chiming bells, marsh marigold—cluster near the water's edge.

You follow the creek up the basin, skirting cliff banks, until a climber's trail veers off to zigzag up the grassy shoulder of the peak you have chosen to climb. By now your heart is racing like a sprinter's, and despite the morning chill you feel sweat under your backpack. You take a water break, then head up the steep trail, forcing yourself to gut it out. The dawn chorus of birds has begun, and you are startled by a flash of indigo, bright as fireworks, as a flock of Western bluebirds suddenly catches the sun's rays.

The high-altitude wildflowers have shrunken into miniature versions of themselves; to really see them, you must stoop to their level, practicing what the locals call "belly botany." Marmots, the alpine cousins of woodchucks, waddle to their lookout posts and whistle reports of your progress to their colleagues higher up.

Soon you leave dirt and grass and begin stepping across a boulder field. Chunks of granite the size of wheelbarrows are decorated by lichen in shades of orange, lime-green, and yellow. You keep your head down, testing each rock for stability before shifting weight to it. Finally, after an hour of rockhopping you reach the ridge, a narrow line of ascent you hope will lead you all the way to the summit. You sling the backpack off and stop to catch your breath. You drink more water, eat a snack. The rush of blood pounding in your ears overwhelms all other sounds. Looking back over your route, you feel accomplished. You'll make the summit, you feel certain.

Down below you see something, a tiny dot just at the edge of timberline. No, two dots. Animals or merely rocks? One spot moves—can't be a rock. A marmot? Size is so hard to judge up here. The second dot looks red. Could they be hikers? You glance skyward, searching for signs of the thunderstorms that roll in before noon. If they are hikers, they're flirting with danger, starting their climb at least three hours late. You watch the ant-crawl progress as the tiny dots edge up the trail.

Then it hits you: from this vantage point, three hours ago you too were a dot like that, a speck of human life on a huge, hulking, weather-creating mountain that has little regard for it. (As a famous climber said, "Mountains don't kill people. They just sit there.") You feel appropriately small, almost insignificant. You get a tiny, fractional glimpse of what God must see all the time.

One of the psalms describes thunder as the voice of the Lord, who strikes the earth with flashes of lightning. We know, of course, that lightning occurs when a positively charged streamer rushes up from the ground to meet a negative charge at the bottom of a cloud. A hundred times a second lightning strikes somewhere on earth, and I for one do not believe God personally programs each course. I have, however, been caught in terrifying storms near the summit of a mountain. With my ice axe humming and my scalp tingling, squatting with feet close together so the charge won't circuit through my body, spaced far enough from my partner to lessen the odds of us both dying, counting the seconds between bolts ("two seconds . . . half a mile")—then, too, I get a glimmer of my true state, a helpless two-legged creature perched on the skin of a molten planet.

I live in daily hope of getting my life under control. At home I left a desk covered with to-do lists: study the manual for my balky printer, unclog pine needles in the gutter, unstick the toilet, change snow tires, check on my sick neighbor. Maybe if I take a day off, I'll have time . . . On the mountain one bolt of lightning, splitting a rock on a nearby peak and exploding against my eardrums, exposes any illusion that I am ever in control. I can count on the moment before me, nothing more.

"Let me know how fleeting is my life," prayed one psalmist. A mountain storm thunderously answers that prayer. The priorities of my life crack apart and slide into a new place.

View from Below

I have had hints of another vantage point that even dwarfs the scale of mountains. One night in 1997 I drove to a lake near my home to watch a lunar eclipse. To the east, hanging just over the mountain peaks, the Hale-Bopp comet lit the sky, brighter far than any star. To judge its size I held my two fists at arm's length, barely covering its luminous, streaming tail. Then I gazed through binoculars at this object that had traveled the breadth of the solar system.

In another corner of the sky, the crescent shadow of earth began crossing the moon, dimming it to an unnatural orangish hue. Mars, closer to earth than it had been in centuries, glowed red above the moon. As the eclipse progressed, all the stars in the sky brightened as if on a rheostat. The Milky Way spilled across the expanse directly above, a broad river of diamond dust. I stood gazing so long that my craned neck grew stiff, and I left only as clouds gathered and snow began to fall, blotting out the celestial view.

I felt appropriately small that night too. To appreciate the scale, consider that if the Milky Way were the size of the entire continent of North America, our solar system would fit in a coffee cup. Even now two Voyager spacecrafts are hurtling toward the edge of the solar system at a rate of 100,000 miles per hour. For almost three decades they have been speeding away from earth, approaching a distance of 9 billion miles. When engineers beam a command to the spacecraft at the speed of light, it takes thirteen hours to arrive. Yet this vast neighborhood of our sun—in truth the size of a coffee cup—fits along with several hundred billion other stars and their minions in the Milky Way, one of perhaps 100 billion such galaxies in the universe. To send a light-speed message to the edge of that universe would take 15 billion years.

"When I consider your heavens, the work of your fingers, the moon and the stars, which you have set in place, what is man that you are mindful of him?" asked the psalmist. An excellent question, as well as a reminder of a point of view I easily forget. We are, we humans, a mere pinch of dust scattered across the surface of a nondescript planet. At the heart of all reality is God, an unimaginable source of both power and love. In the face of such reality we can grovel in humanoid humility or we can, like the psalmist, look up instead of down, to conclude, "O Lord, our Lord, how majestic is your name in all the earth!"

To explore the mystery of prayer I begin here, recalling the vantage I get from the summit of a mountain looking down or from an observatory looking up. Each provides a mere sliver of a glimpse of reality as God must see it. Like a flash of lightning, prayer exposes for a nanosecond what I would prefer to ignore: my own true state of fragile dependence. The undone tasks accumulating at home, my family and every other relation, temptations, health, plans for the future—all these I bring into that larger reality, God's sphere, where I find them curiously upended.

Prayer helps correct myopia, calling to mind a perspective I daily forget. I keep reversing roles, thinking of ways in which God should serve me, rather than vice versa. As God fiercely reminded Job, the Lord of the universe has many things to manage, and in the midst of my self-pity I would do well to contemplate for a moment God's own point of view.

> *Where were you when I laid the earth's foundation?*
>   *Tell me, if you understand.*
> *Who marked off its dimensions? Surely you know!*

Prayer raises my sight beyond the petty—or, as in Job's case, dire—circumstances of daily life to afford a glimpse of that lofty perspective. I realize my tininess and God's vastness, and the true relation of the two. In God's presence I feel small because I am small.

When, after shrugging aside all his caustic theological queries, God enlightened hapless Job, the poor man crumbled. *I'm sorry*, Job said, in effect. *I had no idea what I was asking.* Job did not receive a single answer to his probing questions, a fact that no longer seemed to matter.

> [God asked,] *'Who is this that obscures my counsel without knowledge?'*
> *Surely I spoke of things I did not understand,*
>   *things too wonderful for me to know.*

Kicking and screaming all the way, I am still learning the lesson of Job. God needs no reminding of the nature of reality, but I do.

The third rock from the sun, our planet, has spun off its theological axis. There was a time, Genesis informs us, when God and Adam walked together in the garden and conversed as friends. Nothing seemed more natural for Adam than to commune with the One who had made him, who gave him creative work, who granted his desire for a companion with the lovely gift of Eve. Then, prayer was as natural as conversation with a colleague, or a lover. At the moment of the fall, for Adam and for all who succeeded him, God's presence grew more remote, easier to doubt and even deny.

Every day my vision clouds over so that I perceive nothing but a world of matter. It requires a daily act of will to remember what Paul told the sophisticated crowd in Athens: "[God] is not far from each one of us. For in him we live and move and have our being." For this reason prayer may seem strange, even embarrassing. (How odd, that prayer seems foolish to some people who base their lives on media trends, superstition, instinct, social propriety, or even astrology.)

For most of us, much of the time, prayer brings no certain confirmation we have been heard. We pray in faith that our words somehow cross a bridge between visible and invisible worlds, penetrating a reality of which we have no proof. We enter God's milieu, the realm of spirit, which seems much less real to us than it did to Adam.

Joining the Stream

Jane, a character in Thornton Wilder's play Our Town, got a letter addressed to her farm, town, county, state, and then, the envelope continued, "the United States of America; Continent of North America; Western Hemisphere; the Earth; the Solar System; the Universe; the Mind of God." Perhaps the Christian should reverse the order. If I started with the mind and will of God, viewing the rest of my life from that point of view, other details would fall into place—or at least fall into a different place.

My home sits in a canyon in the shadow of a large mountain along a stream named Bear Creek. During the spring snowmelt and after heavy rains the stream swells, tumbles frothily over rocks, and acts more like a river than a creek. People have drowned in it. Once I traced the origin of Bear Creek to its very source, atop the mountain. I stood on a snowfield marked by "sun cups," the bowl-shaped indentations that form as snow melts. Underneath I could hear a soft gurgling sound, and at the edge of the snow, runnels of water leaked out. These collected into a pool, then a small alpine pond, then spilled over to begin the long journey down the mountain, joining other rivulets to take shape as the creek below my house.

It occurs to me, thinking about prayer, that most of the time I get the direction wrong. I start downstream with my own concerns and bring them to God. I inform God, as if God did not already know. I plead with God, as if hoping to change God's mind and overcome divine reluctance. Instead, I should start upstream where the flow begins.

When I shift direction, I realize that God already cares about my concerns—my uncle's cancer, world peace, a broken family, a rebellious teenager—more than I do. Grace, like water, descends to the lowest part. Streams of mercy flow. I begin with God, who bears primary responsibility for what happens on earth, and ask what part I can play in God's work on earth. "Let justice roll on like a river, righteousness like a never-failing stream!" cried the prophet. Will I stand by the bank or jump in the stream?

With this new starting point for prayer, my perceptions change. I look at nature and see not only wildflowers and golden aspen trees but the signature of a grand artist. I look at human beings and see not only a "poor, bare, forked animal" but a person of eternal destiny made in God's image. Thanksgiving and praise surge up as a natural response, not an obligation.

I need the corrective vision of prayer because all day long I will lose sight of God's perspective. I turn on the television and face a barrage of advertisements assuring me that success and achievement are measured by possessions and physical appearance. Driving downtown, I see a grizzled panhandler holding up a "God bless. Can you help?" sign by the expressway off-ramp, and I avert my eyes. I hear a news report on a dictator in Africa who has just bulldozed entire neighborhoods of squatter homes in an Operation to Drive Out the Trash, leaving 700,000 people homeless. The world obscures the view from above.

WHY PRAY?

Prayer, and only prayer, restores my vision to one that more resembles God's. I awake from blindness to see that wealth lurks as a terrible danger, not a goal worth striving for; that value depends not on race or status but on the image of God a person bears; that no amount of effort to improve physical beauty has much relevance for the world beyond.

Alexander Schmemann, the late priest who led a reform movement in Russian Orthodoxy, tells of a time when he was traveling on the subway in Paris, France, with his fiancée. At one stop an old and ugly woman dressed in the uniform of the Salvation Army got on and found a seat nearby. The two lovers whispered to each other in Russian about how repulsive she looked. A few stops later the woman stood to exit. As she passed them she said in perfect Russian, "I wasn't always ugly." That woman was an angel of God, Schmemann used to tell his students. She opened his eyes, searing his vision in a way he would never forget.

A Habit of Attention

"Be still and know that I am God." I read in this familiar verse from Psalms two commands of equal importance. First, I must be still, something that modern life conspires against. Ten years ago I responded to letters within a couple of weeks and kept my correspondents happy. Five years ago I faxed a response in a couple of days and they seemed content. Now they want email responses the same day and berate me for not using instant messaging or a mobile phone.*

Mystery, awareness of another world, an emphasis on being rather than doing, even a few moments of quiet do not come naturally to me in this hectic, buzzing world. I must carve out time and allow God to nourish my inner life.

---

* When a journalist asked Thomas Merton to diagnose the leading spiritual disease of our time, the monk gave a curious one-word answer: efficiency. Why? "From the monastery to the Pentagon, the plant has to run . . . and there is little time or energy left over after that to do anything else."

On a walking pilgrimage to Assisi in Italy, the writer Patricia Hampl began to make a list in answer to the question, What is prayer? She wrote down a few words. Praise. Gratitude. Begging/pleading/cutting deals. Fruitless whining and puling. Focus. And then the list broke off, for she discovered that prayer only seems like an act of language: "Fundamentally it is a position, a placement of oneself." She went on to discover that "prayer as focus is not a way of limiting what can be seen; it is a habit of attention brought to bear on all that is."

Ah, a habit of attention. Be still. In that focus, all else comes into focus. In that rift in my routine, the universe falls into alignment.

Stillness prepares me for the second command: "know that I am God; I will be exalted among the nations, I will be exalted in the earth." Only through prayer can I believe that truth in the midst of a world that colludes to suppress, not exalt, God.

In testimony given before the Truth and Reconciliation Commission hearings in South Africa, one black man told of crying out to God as the white officers attached electrodes to his body after beating him with truncheons. They laughed in his face: "We are God here," jeered one of the guards. The Commission hearings bared the delusion of that brash claim, for the guards, stripped of all power, now sat in a defendants' box with heads bowed as their accusers paraded before them. They had been dethroned.

Psalm 2 depicts God laughing in the heavens, scoffing at the kings and rulers arrayed in revolt. For the South African prisoner, or a pastor harassed in China, or believers persecuted in North Korea, it requires a great leap to attain that sublime faith, to believe that God is indeed exalted among the nations.* I think of Paul *singing* in a Philippian jail

---

* A seventeenth-century prayer from the British House of Commons gets the right perspective, in words that sound eerily foreign in today's political climate: "Almighty God, by whom alone Kings reign, and Princes decree justice; and from whom alone cometh all counsel, wisdom and understanding; We thine unworthy servants, here gathered together in thy Name, do most humbly beseech thee to send down thy heavenly wisdom from above, to direct and guide us in all our consultations; And grant that we, having thy fear always before our eyes, and laying aside all private interests, prejudices, and partial affections, the result of all our counsels, may be the glory of thy blessed name."

and of Jesus correcting Pilate with the plain truth, "You would have no power over me if it were not given to you from above." Even at that moment of crisis, Jesus had the long view, the view from a time antedating the solar system.

"Be still and know that I am God": the Latin imperative for "be still" is *vacate*. As Simon Tugwell explains, "God invites us to take a holiday [*vacation*], to stop being God for a while, and let him be God." Too often we think of prayer as a serious chore, something that must be scheduled around other appointments, shoehorned in among other pressing activities. We miss the point, says Tugwell. "God is inviting us to take a break, to play truant. We can stop doing all those important things we have to do in our capacity as God, and leave it to him to be God." Prayer allows me to admit my failures, weaknesses, and limitations to One who responds to human vulnerability with infinite mercy.

To let God be God, of course, means climbing down from my own executive chair of control. I must "uncreate" the world I have so carefully fashioned to further my ends and advance my cause. Adam and Eve, the builders of Babel, Nebuchadnezzar, the South African guards, not to mention all who struggle with addictions or even ego, know well what is at stake. If original sin traces back to two people striving to become like God, the first step in prayer is to acknowledge or "remember" God—to restore the truth of the universe. "That Man may know he dwell not in his own," said Milton.

Aliens

For several years I have tried to help a Japanese family, the Yokotas, in their desperate search for justice. In 1977 their thirteen-year-old daughter Megumi vanished on her way home from badminton practice after school. Police dogs tracked her scent to a nearby beach, but the distraught Yokotas had no clues that might explain their daughter's sudden disappearance.

Sixteen years later, long after the Yokotas had resigned themselves to Megumi's death, a North Korean defector made a stunning claim: a Japanese woman named Megumi, who played badminton, was living in North Korea at a training institute for intelligence agents. Scores of Japanese, he said, had been kidnapped and forced to teach Korean spies the Japanese language and culture. He provided heartrending details of Megumi's abduction: agents had seized her, wrapped her in a straw mat, and rowed her to a waiting spy ship, where she had spent the night scratching against the hold with bloody fingers, crying "Mother!"

For years North Korea dismissed all such reports as fabrications. But in the face of mounting pressure, Kim Jong-il himself, the "Dear Leader" of North Korea, at long last admitted to the abduction of thirteen Japanese, including Megumi. Five returned to Japan, but North Koreans insisted the other eight had died, including Megumi who, they said, in 1993 had used a kimono to hang herself. Much information supplied by North Korea proved false, however, and the Yokotas refused to believe the reports of their daughter's death. All over Japan, prayer groups sprang up to support the abductees. Mrs. Yokota traveled across the globe in her quest for justice, becoming in the process one of the most familiar faces on Japanese media.

In 2004, twenty-seven years after the abduction, the North Koreans gave Megumi's parents three photos of their daughter. The most poignant, taken just after her capture, shows her at age thirteen still in her Japanese schoolgirl's uniform, looking unbearably forlorn. "We couldn't help crying when we saw the picture," her mother tearfully told reporters. Two other photos showed her as an adult, a woman in her thirties standing outdoors in a winter coat.

The Yokotas fondled the photos over and over, finding some solace in the fact that the later photos showed their daughter looking healthy and reasonably well-cared-for. They tried to imagine Megumi's life. Had she met with other abductees and conversed with them to keep from forgetting her mother tongue? What had helped her remember who she was: not an immigrant to North Korea but a Japanese taken captive against her will? Had she tried to sneak a message back to them? Attempted an escape? What memories did she retain of her life in Japan, life as their daughter? How many times had Megumi looked toward the island of Japan and scoured newspapers in search of clues of her former home?

On a trip to Asia in 2004, I was asked to speak to the combined prayer groups in Tokyo. I agonized over what I might say to bring comfort to the family and concerned friends. I turned to the Bible in search of anything that might relate to the Yokotas' predicament, and made a list of characters who had served God in foreign lands: Abram departing for a new homeland that included Sodom and Gomorrah; Joseph abducted, presumed dead, then rising to prominence in Egypt; Daniel and other prophets serving enemy administrations in Babylon (Iraq) and then Persia (Iran); Esther risking her life to preserve her compatriots in Persia; Paul taking the gospel to Rome in chains, forerunner of a host of missionaries who would encounter resistance from foreign cultures, including many early martyrs in Japan itself.

All these, like Megumi, must have struggled to retain a memory of who they were: aliens swept into a new and strange culture. The prophet Daniel defied a tyrant's orders by opening his window and praying three times a day toward his home city of Jerusalem. For him, for the other believers living in foreign lands, and perhaps for Megumi as well, prayer was the main reminder of a reality contradicted by all surroundings. A channel of faith, it served to restore the truth belied by everything around them.

For us, too, prayer can be that channel. We live on a broken planet, fallen far from God's original intent. It takes effort to remember who we are, God's creation, and faith to imagine what we someday will be, God's triumph.

Why pray? I have asked this question almost every day of my Christian life, especially when God's presence seems far away and I wonder if prayer is a pious form of talking to myself. I have asked it when I read theology, wondering what use there may be in repeating what God must surely know. My conclusions will unfold only gradually, but I begin here because prayer has become for me much more than a shopping list of requests to present to God. It has become a realignment of everything. I pray to restore the truth of the universe, to gain a glimpse of the world, and of me, through the eyes of God.

In prayer I shift my point of view away from my own selfishness. I climb above timberline and look down at the speck that is myself. I gaze at the stars and recall what role I or any of us play in a universe beyond comprehension. Prayer is the act of seeing reality from God's point of view.

∼ Why Pray?

Prayers like gravel
flung at the sky's
window, hoping to attract
the loved one's
attention . . .

— R. S. THOMAS

DOES GOD REALLY CARE about the details of our lives, such as getting a house sold or finding a lost cat? And if the answer is yes, then what about a hurricane that flattens a city or a tsunami that washes away a quarter million people? Why does God seem so capricious in deciding if and when to intervene on this chaotic planet?

Prayers of request tend to fall into one of two categories: trouble or trivia. As if by instinct we cry out to God when trouble strikes. A parent hovering over a sick child, a frightened airplane passenger, a sailor caught in a lightning storm—we call upon God when in danger, sometimes with an appeal no more articulate than "Oh, God!" At that moment, forget any lofty notion of keeping company with God. I want help from some Power greater than I. "There are no atheists in fox-holes," Army chaplains like to say.

We also pray for trivial things. In Tolstoy's *War and Peace* a hunter prays earnestly that the hunted wolf might come in his direction. "Why not grant me this?" he asks God. "I know Thou art great and that it's wrong to pray about this; but for God's sake make the old wolf come my way and let Karay [a dog] spring at it—in front of 'Uncle' who is watching from over there—and fix his teeth in its throat and finish it off!"

In part to put behind him the bitter taste of divorce, a friend of mine traveled to South America and visited a national park. He prayed diligently, with all the right motives he assured me, to see some rare mammals and snakes. To increase the odds he stayed awake during the night and even spent twenty hours on a mosquito-ridden treetop platform. Others in the eco-tour group happened across rare mammals by chance, while time and again my friend just missed seeing them. He returned from the trip wondering if God ever intervenes: neither his urgent prayers against the divorce nor his worshipful prayers to appreciate the wonders of nature met an answer.

Of course, if our trivial prayers do get answered—if Tolstoy's wolf had walked toward Rostov and a menagerie of indigenous mammals had paraded before my friend's spotting tower—that raises other, serious problems. As one philosophy professor put it, "If God can influence the course of events, then a God who is willing to cure colds and provide parking spaces but is not willing to prevent Auschwitz and Hiroshima is morally repugnant. Since Hiroshima and Auschwitz did occur, one must infer that God cannot (or has a policy never to) influence the course of worldly events."

Even for one who rejects the professor's extreme conclusion, the haunting questions linger.

What Is the Point?

Not wanting to treat prayer as an abstraction, I opened a file drawer and read through letters I have received from readers of my books. They pose questions about prayer not in the abstract but personally, often poignantly.

A prisoner wrote from Indiana, "God's overall supervision of creation is scripturally clear, but does He concern himself at all, to the point of intervention, in our daily trivial lives? Or are His promises of help aimed only at our spiritual self, to help how we respond to events, not to affect events themselves?" He mentioned his own troubling circumstances—his incarceration, a sister in divorce proceedings, a girlfriend jilting him— and then told of an inner-city family he stays close to.

> The teen son has endured chronic asthma, a touch of cerebral palsy, physical abuse by his father, shame for his various disabilities and, finally, the murder of his mother. Something's wrong when all that can happen to innocents like them, especially when Jesus spoke so poignantly about His protection for the meek and doing good to "the least of these." I keep going back to the scene where I drove that teen out to find his mother's grave site only to discover that his relatives hadn't been rich enough to buy a headstone. Begging God's intervention in *any* part of those sad people's lives would not be considered a request for frivolous magic but the merest mercy.

The prisoner had read about filmmaker Francis Ford Coppolla, who directed one of his movies entirely from a remote trailer, watching the proceedings through a bank of monitors and communicating with the actors through a microphone and headsets. "Does God run the world like that?" he asked.

Another reader, from Idaho, described his struggles with prayer as middle-class whinings about such things as college debts, poor money management, marriage struggles, a failing business, an aging father. The tone of the letter quickened, though, when he mentioned his son, who because of a stroke at birth had grown up with a severely deformed foot and a useless hand. "We pray daily for his body to be healed," wrote the father. Does God care about such matters? Most of us have secret desires—if not for healing, then for success, happiness, security, peace. "Do we dare ask God for some of these things? . . . I'm looking for a road that I can walk on, and teach my son."

A woman, age forty-one, wrote first about her conversion as a Jewish believer in Jesus, and then of a daunting trial, breast cancer that had spread to lungs and liver. Sometimes she would pull away from God completely, but then "after sulking in silence for a period of days or weeks, I would come back to God slowly and reluctantly, a pout still on my face, but recognizing that I didn't know how to live apart from God." Throughout the long ordeal, she agonized over how to pray.

> What is the point of praying for something to happen? I can understand the point of praying as a means of simply trying to establish communion with God. But why should I pray for someone to be healed or for my husband to get a job or for my parents to come to salvation? I pray for others because I often feel helpless to do anything else, and I cling to hope that maybe, just maybe this time it will matter.
>
> My spiritual leaders are always admonishing our congregation to spend hours in prayer, interceding for those in need. Why, if God has plans and knows what we want and need and what's best for us, should I spend hours asking him to change his mind? And how do I pray with faith when it seems that the kind of prayer I am lifting up rarely gets answered?

She told of the hundreds of people who were praying for her healing from cancer, and wondered whether their prayers mattered. "Am I more likely to get healed than my friend who also has cancer but has only a handful of people regularly praying for her? I sometimes joke that God has got to heal me or he will have to answer to every one of those people who is praying for me." She teaches an elementary class in a Christian school and one day gave this assignment: If you met Jesus walking down the street, what would you ask him? Most of the students wrote questions of curiosity: "What is heaven like?" and "How was it when you were a kid?" One student wrote, "Why won't you heal my mom?" and "Why doesn't my dad find a job?" With a pang, she recognized the student's handwriting—her own son's.

The most disturbing letter spoke of the fresh wound of an unanswered prayer. For years two parents had prayed for protection for their emotionally troubled son. One day they got a call from their daughter, who had just found the young man, age twenty-two, dead of carbon monoxide poisoning. The letter recorded their simple response to God: "Lord, we prayed regularly for all three of our children—didn't You hear our prayers?" Then the mother wrote out some of her favorite verses from the Bible: "Ask whatever you wish and it will be given to you. . . . I will never leave you, I will never forsake you. . . . My grace is sufficient. . . . In all things God works for the good of those who love Him." How could she reconcile those verses with her son's suicide?

Jesus at Prayer

Although I replied to each of these letters, doing so left me with more questions than answers. All that follows—indeed the very existence of this book—flows out of my search for answers, and I will approach these questions from different angles as I circle around the mystery of prayer. What can I discover about prayer that might somehow offer consolation?

As a starting point I take the real-life stories of a prisoner, a middle-class man from Idaho, a forty-one-year-old breast cancer survivor, and a family devastated by suicide and look for insights from the first-century rabbi who changed the world. Surely Jesus must have known the potential as well as the limitations of prayer. I have said that the simplest answer to the question "Why pray?" is "Because Jesus did." What relevance might Jesus' prayers have for the people who wrote me letters?

The Gospels record just over a dozen specific prayers by Jesus, along with several parables and teachings on the subject. He followed the normal Jewish practice of visiting the synagogue, the "house of prayer," and of praying at least three times a day. We can safely assume that Jesus also prayed in private, for when his disciples asked for instruction on prayer Jesus said they should seclude themselves. Such prayers in solitude made an impression on his followers: five times the Gospels mention Jesus' practice of praying alone.

WHY PRAY?

Like most of us, Jesus turned to prayer in times of trouble. No doubt he prayed intensely as he fasted and meditated on the Bible during his time of wilderness tempting. He prayed aloud as the rendezvous with death approached, the words expressing his inner turmoil: "Now my heart is troubled, and what shall I say? 'Father, save me from this hour'? No, it was for this very reason I came to this hour." His prayers in the garden of Gethsemane pushed him to the edge of endurance, and three times he fell to the ground, overcome. Jesus' prayers held back nothing.

Two of the prayers in troubled times (the *Abba* in Gethsemane and *Eloi* from the cross) were so moving that words from the original Semitic language stuck in the minds of hearers. Of the seven cries Jesus cried out from the cross, at least three were prayers. Hebrews reports that "he offered up prayers and petitions with loud cries and tears to the one who could save him from death"—but of course he was not saved from death. Like the people who wrote me letters, like all of us at times, Jesus knew the sensation of getting no answer to his pleas.

The other typical form of request, prayer for trivial things, apparently had little place in Jesus' practice. Common, everyday things, yes: the Lord's Prayer mentions daily bread, temptations, and broken relationships, but these requests are hardly trivial. Jesus' prayers, in fact, show a remarkable lack of concern about his own needs. "Take this cup from me" may represent the only time Jesus asked something for himself.

If he made few requests on his own behalf, Jesus often lifted up prayers for others. He prayed for children brought to him by their mothers, and for "the people standing here" at Lazarus's grave side, and for Simon Peter who faced a time of testing. In his final intercessory prayer, one last gasp of grace, he asked on behalf of his persecutors, "Father, forgive them, for they do not know what they are doing."

When alone, Jesus relied on prayer as a kind of spiritual recharging. After an exhausting day of ministry—recruiting disciples, preaching to crowds, healing the sick—he would withdraw to an isolated place to pray. The tempter had used the lure of popularity and acclaim to test him in the wilderness, and perhaps Jesus needed to escape the clamor in order to firm up his resistance and renew his sense of mission. "I have food to eat that you know nothing about," he reassured his disciples, who worried about his lack of nourishment at such times.

Jesus' prayers intensified around key events—his baptism, an all-night session before choosing his twelve disciples, on the Mount of Transfiguration—and especially as he prepared for his departure. Once, he burst into an exuberant prayer when a large group of his followers on a short-term mission returned with tales of spiritual triumph. He prayed for his disciples that the Holy Spirit would come as a "Counselor to be with you forever." In one long, magnificent prayer recorded in John 17, he prayed not only for the immediate disciples but for all of us through-out history who would believe in him because of their message.

Does Prayer Matter?

After surveying Jesus' practice of prayer, I realize that his example does answer one important question about prayer: Does it matter? When doubts creep in and I wonder whether prayer is a sanctified form of talk-ing to myself, I remind myself that the Son of God, who had spoken worlds into being and sustains all that exists, felt a compelling need to pray. He prayed as if it made a difference, as if the time he devoted to prayer mattered every bit as much as the time he devoted to caring for people.

A physician friend of mine who learned I was investigating prayer told me I would have to start with three rather large assumptions: (1) God exists; (2) God is capable of hearing our prayers; and (3) God cares about our prayers. "None of these three can be proved or disproved," he said. "They must either be believed or disbelieved." He is right, of course, although for me the example of Jesus offers strong evidence in favor of that belief. To discount prayer, to conclude that it does not mat-ter, means to view Jesus as deluded.

In keeping with his race, Jesus truly believed that prayer could change things. Romans of the time prayed to their gods as one would finger a good luck charm, not really expecting much. The skeptical Greeks derided prayer, their playwrights weaving foolish, ridiculous, and even obscene prayers into their plays to provoke the audience to uproarious laughter. Only the stubborn Jews, despite their tragic history of unanswered prayers, contended that a supreme and loving God ruled the earth, listened to their prayers, and would someday respond.

Jesus claimed to be part of that response, the fulfillment of the Jewish longing for Messiah. "Anyone who has seen me has seen the Father," he once said, and went about exhibiting the will of the Father by feeding the hungry, healing the sick, and liberating the captives. When I get letters from people with intractable problems, I tell them I cannot answer the "Why?" questions. I can, though, answer another question, and that is how God feels about their plight. We know how God feels, because Jesus gave us a face, one sometimes streaked with tears. We can follow Jesus through the Gospels and see how he responds to a widow who has lost her son, to an outcast woman whose bleeding won't stop, even to a Roman officer whose servant has fallen ill. In his tender mercy Jesus gave us a visible sign of how the Father must hear our prayers even now.

"Your will be done on earth as it is in heaven," Jesus taught us to pray, and he of all people knew the contrast between the two places. On earth Jesus daily confronted tokens of opposition to that will. Mothers thrust sick babies toward him, beggars called out, widows grieved, demons mocked him, enemies stalked him. In such an alien environment, he turned to prayer both as a refuge from mewling crowds and as a reminder of his true home, a place that had no room for evil, pain, and death.

Jesus clung to prayer as to a lifeline, for it gave him both the guidance and the energy to know and do the Father's will. To maintain belief in the "real" world from which he came, to nourish memory of eternal light, he had to work at it all night on occasion or rise before daybreak. Even then he sometimes grew exasperated with his earthly surroundings ("O unbelieving generation, how long shall I stay with you?"), sometimes fought temptation ("Do not put the Lord your God to the test"), and sometimes doubted ("My God, my God, why have you forsaken me?").

Skeptics raise questions about prayer's usefulness: If God knows best, what's the point? As one pastor asked me, "Should I just stop bothering him with my petty requests for myself and others, and let God get on with the business of running the universe while I do my best to take care of things down here?"* To such questions, I have no better answer than the example of Jesus, who knew above any of us the wisdom of the Father and yet who felt a strong need to flood the heavens with requests.

Although Jesus offered no metaphysical proofs of the effectiveness of prayer, the very fact that he did it establishes its worth. "Ask and you will receive," he said frankly, a rebuke to anyone who considers petition a "primitive" form of prayer. When his disciples failed in their attempts to heal the afflicted boy, Jesus had a simple explanation: lack of prayer.

Prayer Limits

And yet, it appears, prayer was no simple matter even for Jesus. I once wrote an article titled "Jesus' Unanswered Prayers," and it gave me wistful comfort to review the record of Jesus' prayers and find that in respect to prayer, too, he fully shared the human condition. Like the people who write me letters, he knows the heartbreak of unanswered prayers. His longest prayer, after all, centers in a request for unity, "that all of them may be one, Father, just as you are in me and I am in you." The slightest acquaintance with church history (at recent count 34,000 distinct denominations and sects) shows how far that prayer remains from being answered.

I included in my list of problematic prayers the night when Jesus sought guidance for choosing the twelve disciples whom he would

---

* The philosopher Rousseau had a similar explanation for why he did not pray: "Why should I ask of him that he would change for me the course of things? — I who ought to love, above all, the order established by his wisdom and maintained by his Providence, shall I wish that order to be dissolved on my account?"

entrust with his mission. "Jesus went out to a mountainside to pray, and spent the night praying to God," Luke records. "When morning came, he called his disciples to him and chose twelve of them, whom he also designated apostles." Yet as I read the Gospels I marvel that this dodgy dozen could constitute the answer to any prayer. They included, Luke pointedly notes, "Judas Iscariot, who became a traitor," not to mention the ambitious Sons of Thunder and the hothead Simon, whom Jesus would once address as "Satan." When Jesus later sighed in exasperation over these twelve, "How long shall I put up with you?" I wonder if he momentarily questioned the Father's guidance back on the mountainside.

In his provocative book *The Gospel According to Judas*, theologian Ray Anderson ponders Jesus' selection of Judas as one of the twelve. Did Jesus foresee Judas's destiny the night he prayed? Did he remind the Father of that prayer as Judas left the Last Supper table to betray him? Anderson draws from the experience of Judas a key principle about prayer: "Prayer is not a means of removing the unknown and unpredictable elements in life, but rather a way of including the unknown and unpredictable in the outworking of the grace of God in our lives."

Jesus' own prayers for his disciples surely did not remove the "unknown and unpredictable elements." The twelve periodically surprised and disappointed Jesus with their petty concerns and their inadequate faith. In the end, all twelve failed him at the hour of his deepest need. Eventually, however, eleven of the twelve underwent a slow but steady transformation, providing a kind of long-term answer to Jesus' original prayer. John, a Son of Thunder, softened into "the apostle of Love." Simon Peter, who earned Jesus' rebuke by recoiling from the idea of Messiah suffering, later showed how to "follow in his steps" by suffering as Christ did. The one exception, Judas, betrayed Jesus and yet that very act led to the cross and the salvation of the world. In strange and mysterious ways, prayer incorporates the unknown and unpredictable in the outworking of God's grace.

Although Jesus' prayers do not offer a foolproof formula, they do give clues as to how God works—and does not work—on this planet. Especially when trouble strikes, we want God to intervene more decisively, but Jesus' prayers underscore God's style of restraint out of respect for human freedom. Often God rules by overruling.

One scene in particular shows the built-in limitations of prayer. "Simon, Simon, Satan has asked to sift you as wheat," Jesus informed Peter, pointedly using his old name. "But I have prayed for you, Simon, that your faith may not fail." With characteristic bluster Peter insisted he would follow Jesus to prison and to death, and it was then Jesus revealed the ugly truth that actually Peter would deny him three times before the rooster crowed that same day. I cannot help wondering why Jesus didn't flat-out deny Satan's request to test Simon: "No, he's off limits. You can't touch him!" Or why didn't Jesus miraculously embolden Peter so that he could withstand the sifting? Instead he chose the more subtle tack of praying that Peter's faith not fail.

Of course, Peter's faith did fail, three times. Does this request belong in the list of Jesus' unanswered prayers? Or does it, rather, hint at the underlying pattern of how God operates on earth? The scene with Peter has fascinating parallels with the account of Judas. There too, a trusted disciple failed a test of faith, with consequences that seemed catastrophic. Luke, as if trying to explain how such treachery could happen, reports simply, "Then Satan entered Judas." How else to explain such a deed?

Judas and Peter both got caught up in a drama of spiritual warfare that they could neither recognize nor fathom. Satan directly pursued both disciples, yet each bore a measure of personal responsibility, for Satan conquers no one without cooperation. Both men miserably failed their test of faith, betraying a master they had followed for three years. Nonetheless, even after their failure both faced the possibility of redemption. One realized his error and hung himself. The other realized his error, repented, and became a pillar of the church. Is it possible that Jesus' prayer for Peter kept him from becoming another Judas? And what might Jesus have prayed for Judas—he who taught us to pray for our persecutors and himself did so from the cross? Their last scene together has Jesus saying to Judas, "Friend, do what you came for."

Peter's testing faintly echoes the plot of Job: Satan asks permission to work mischief, God grants it and then, showing puzzling restraint, waits to see how the tested human will respond. Peter, like Job, like everyone, had the freedom to pass or fail the test. Jesus adds one more factor: his own fervent prayer on Peter's behalf. The working out of this plot, in people like Job, Judas, and Peter, throws light on the great puzzle of human history. Why does God "sit on his hands" while Satan works mischief, while evil tyrants oppress good people, while a traitor delivers God's own Son to the enemy?

The Bible makes a strong contrast between the freedom-crushing style of evil and the freedom-respecting style of good. In a vivid scene of possession by an evil spirit, Mark 9 shows a young boy foaming at the mouth, gnashing his teeth, and throwing himself into fire or water. In every way evil possession transforms the boy into a caricature of a human being, forcibly overwhelming human freedom. Contrast that scene with possession by the Holy Spirit. Paul warns, "Quench not the Spirit" and "grieve not the holy Spirit of God." The Lord of the universe becomes so small, so freedom-respecting as to put himself somehow at our mercy.

Words fail to capture the enormity of descent when a sovereign God takes up residence in a person and says, in effect, "Don't hurt me. Don't push me away." The poet John Donne prayed, "Batter my heart, three-person'd God." But God rarely does. God woos, and waits.

Jesus' prayers for Peter—and perhaps for Judas as well—express God's unfathomable respect for human freedom. Even when he senses his close friend will betray him, Jesus does not intervene with a freedom-crushing miracle. He allows history to take its course, at enormous personal cost, praying all the while that even betrayal and death may be redeemed as part of the outworking of the grace of God. For Peter's sake, for Judas's, and for the world's, that prayer found an answer.

Unprayed Prayers

I learn as much from the prayers Jesus did *not* pray as from those he did. These, too, underscore God's mysterious style of working on this planet. When his cousin John faced imprisonment and certain execution, Jesus did not pray for his release and miraculous delivery—just as he did not pray that Satan keep hands off Peter, nor that Judas change his mind.

And, in a tantalizing aside, Jesus reprimanded Peter for his violent resistance in Gethsemane: "Do you think I cannot call on my Father, and he will at once put at my disposal more than twelve legions of angels?" A Roman legion comprised 6,000 soldiers, which means Jesus chose not to pray for 72,000 celestial reinforcements at the moment of his arrest! Judas and Peter both heard the bold claim, but evidently neither believed it, Judas proceeding with his treachery and Peter fleeing into the darkness.

As a result of Jesus' unprayed prayer, instead of movies depicting a sky full of warrior-angels and ferocious cosmic combat, we get Mel Gibson's movie of a solitary figure whose body is lashed into shreds of skin. What if Jesus had prayed that prayer? How would history have changed? Jesus could have put an end to evil—and to all human history, for that matter—by praying for heavenly rescue forces, but he elected not to. Instead of a triumphant victory by force, he opted for a much more arduous (for him and for the rest of us) path to redemption.

All who struggle with God can look back to that dark night when the Son of God himself struggled with the Father.

"Abba, Father," he said, "everything is possible for you." *Ah, there is a way out. I need not endure the pain and humiliation after all. Everything is indeed possible. Legions of angels await my command.*

"Take this cup from me." *There, I've said it. The unprayed prayer has passed my lips. I give in, give up. I cannot bear the future, cannot bear the present. There must be some other way. I beg you, Father, if there is any other way . . .*

"Yet not what I will, but what you will." *More than anything, I will rescue and deliverance from the enemy. That is what you will also—only not just for me but for the world. We cannot have one without surrendering the other and that, of course, is why I came. Therefore I yield. Your greater, more costly will, Father, becomes mine.*

In that struggle, by all accounts an authentic one of sweat and blood and ardent appeals to heaven, Jesus' fate was sealed—by his own choice. Astonishingly, a spirit of tranquility carried him through everything that followed: the trials before the Sanhedrin, Herod, and Pilate, the beatings, the torture, the crucifixion itself. Mel Gibson's *The Passion of the Christ* does not always depict it that way, but in the Gospels' accounts Jesus is the least intimidated, most composed character on the scene. When he volunteers himself to the arresting guards, they draw back and fall to the ground. Jesus is calling the shots, as he reminds Pilate: "You would have no power over me if it were not given to you from above."

For most of us prayer serves as a resource to help in a time of testing or conflict. For Jesus, it was the battle itself. Once the Gethsemane prayers had aligned him with the Father's will, what happened next was merely the means to fulfill it. Prayer mattered that much. In the words of Haddon Robinson,

> Where was it that Jesus sweat great drops of blood? Not in Pilate's Hall, nor on his way to Golgotha. It was in the Garden of Gethsemane. There he "offered up prayers and petitions with loud cries and tears to the One who could save him from death" (Hebrews 5:7). Had I been there and witnessed that struggle, I would have worried about the future. "If he is so broken up when all he is doing is praying," I might have said, "what will he do when he faces a real crisis? Why can't he approach this ordeal with the calm confidence of his three sleeping friends?" Yet, when the test came, Jesus walked to the cross with courage, and his three friends fell apart and fell away.

Parental Pain

In the end, what can I learn from Jesus' example about how prayer works? More to the point, what can I tell the people whose letters I quoted early in this chapter? I wish I could tell them that the Lord's Prayer would find a speedier answer—that God's will shall soon be done on this earth as it is in heaven. I believe in miracles, but I also believe they are *miracles*, meaning rare exceptions to the normal laws that govern the planet. I cannot, nor can anyone, promise that prayer will solve all problems and eliminate all suffering. At the same time, I also know that Jesus commanded his followers to pray, certain that it makes a difference in a world full of opposition to God's will.

For whatever reason, God now tolerates a world in which fathers abuse their physically disabled sons, children live with congenital birth defects, breast cancers metastasize, and distressed young people commit suicide. Why does God so rarely step in and bring miraculous intervention to our prayer requests? Why is suffering distributed so randomly and unfairly? No one knows the complete answer to those questions. For a time, God has chosen to operate on this broken planet mostly from the bottom up rather than from the top down—a pattern that God's own Son subjected himself to on earth. Partly out of respect for human freedom, God often allows things to play out "naturally."

Even so, God surely feels the same compassion for human suffering that Jesus demonstrated as he walked among us. When Jesus looked out over the city of Jerusalem, knowing what its leaders had in store for him, he cried out, "O Jerusalem, Jerusalem, you who kill the prophets and stone those sent to you, how often I have longed to gather your children together, as a hen gathers her chicks under her wings, but you were not willing." Though not a parent, he knew well the helpless state of loving parents who watch their children make self-destructive choices. As I pray, I keep before me the compassionate face of Jesus.

Jesus knew, too, the cost of divine restraint, the deeply personal cost of letting the world have its way with him. He understood that redemption comes from passing through the pain, not avoiding it: "for the joy set before him [he] endured the cross." Somehow redeemed suffering is better than no suffering at all, Easter better than skipping Good Friday altogether. Although Jesus knew the redemptive pattern in advance—he had revealed it to his disciples—how remote it must have seemed to him in the garden and on the *via dolorosa*. How remote it seems to all of us in the midst of our trials.

Jesus' prayer for Peter shows the same pattern in sharp relief. Satan partially got his way with Peter, sifting him like wheat. But in answer to Jesus' prayer, the sifting rid Peter of his least attractive qualities: blustery self-confidence, a chip on his shoulder, a propensity to violence. The Gospels show Peter urging Jesus to avoid the cross, cowering in the darkness the night of Jesus' trial, and denying with an oath that he knows him. In the book of 1 Peter a transformed apostle uses words like *humble* and *submit*, and welcomes suffering as a badge of honor.

God has not leashed the forces of evil, not yet anyway,* but has provided resources beyond our awareness, including the personal concern of the Son, to counter and even transform evil. We know that prayer matters because after leaving earth Jesus made it one of his primary tasks: "Therefore he is able to save completely those who come to God through him, because he always lives to intercede for them." As Jesus once prayed for Peter, now he prays for us, including all those whose letters I quoted. In fact, the New Testament's only glimpse of what Jesus is doing right now depicts him at the right hand of God "interceding for us." In three years of active ministry, Jesus changed the moral landscape of the planet. For nearly two thousand years since, he has been using another tactic: prayer.

When I betray the love and grace God has shown me, I fall back on the promise that Jesus prays for me—as he did for Peter—not that I

---

* The Bible promises that this style of working is temporary. Contrast Jesus' prayer for Peter with this prediction of how Jesus will handle evil in the future: "And then the lawless one will be revealed, whom the Lord Jesus will overthrow with the breath of his mouth and destroy by the splendor of his coming."

would never face testing, nor ever fail, but that in the end I will allow God to use the testing and failure to mold me into someone more useful to the kingdom, someone more like Jesus.

⁓ Ask, Seek, Knock

. . . And if by prayer
Incessant I could hope to change the will
Of Him who all things can, I would not cease
To weary him with my assiduous cries.

—JOHN MILTON

JESUS' STORY ABOUT VILLAGE neighbors must have provoked smiles and chuckles in his first-century audience. A man opens his door to an unexpected guest late one night—not uncommon in a desert climate that encourages travel after sunset—only to find his pantry bare. In a region renowned for hospitality, no decent person would turn away a weary traveler or put him to bed without nourishment, so the host strikes out to a friend's house to ask for bread.

Kenneth Bailey, a Presbyterian missionary who lived in Lebanon forty years, illuminates some of the cultural nuances behind the story. Palestinians use bread as Westerners use silverware: they break off bite-sized pieces, dip into a common dish of meat and vegetables, and eat the entire sop. The man with empty cupboards was likely asking his friend for a main course as well as loaves of bread, and even that was typical. Villagers frequently borrowed from each other in hospitality emergencies. Bailey recalls one instance: "While living in primitive Middle Eastern villages, we discovered to our amazement that this custom of rounding up from the neighbors something adequate for the guest extended even to us when we were the guests. We would accept an invitation to a meal

49

clear across the village, and arrive to eat from our own dishes which the villagers had borrowed quietly from our cook."

In Jesus' story, though, the neighbor stubbornly refuses the request (see Luke 11). He has already gone to bed, stretched out with his family on a mat in the one-room house—and, besides, the door is bolted shut. "Don't bother me," he calls to his neighbor outside. "I can't get up and give you anything."

A Middle Eastern audience would have laughed out loud at this lame excuse. Can you imagine such a neighbor? Jesus was asking. *Certainly not! No one in my village would act so rudely. If he did, the entire village would know about it by morning!*

Then Jesus delivers the punch line: "I tell you, though he will not get up and give him the bread because he is his friend, yet because of the man's boldness [his *persistence*, his *shamelessness*] he will get up and give him as much as he needs." The application to prayer follows immediately: "So I say to you: Ask and it will be given to you; seek and you will find; knock and the door will be opened to you."

Luke positions this story right after Jesus' teaching on the Lord's Prayer, drawing a sharp contrast between the reluctant neighbor and God the Father. If a cranky neighbor who has turned in for the night, who wishes more than anything you would go away, who does his best to ignore you—if such a neighbor eventually rouses to give what you want, how much more will God respond to your bold persistence in prayer! After all, what earthly father would sneak a snake under his son's pillow when he asks for a fish, or drop a scorpion on his daughter's breakfast plate instead of an egg?

The Lord's Prayer, often reduced to a mumbled ritual, an incantation, takes on new light in this story abutting it. We should pray like a salesman with his foot wedged in the door opening, like a wrestler who has his opponent in a headlock and won't let go.

The God "who watches over you will not slumber," promises a psalm of comfort. Even so, sometimes when we pray it feels as if God has indeed nodded off. Raise your voice, Jesus' story implies. Strive on, like the shameless neighbor in the middle of the night. Keep pounding the door.

Battering the Gates

A few chapters later Luke records another charming story, this time featuring a nagging widow as the unlikely heroine. Some of Jesus' parables left his disciples scratching their heads, but this one came with an unmistakable point: "to show them that they should always pray and not give up." The story takes the even riskier step of comparing God to a callous, corrupt judge who has to listen to the widow's loud grievance.

Today, many cities have a free legal aid clinic to help poor and underserved clients negotiate a confusing system of courts and depositions. To illustrate the very different situation in Jesus' day, Kenneth Bailey cites a scene witnessed by a Western traveler in nineteenth-century Iraq:

> On a slightly raised dais . . . sat the *Kadi*, or judge, half buried in cushions. Round him squatted various secretaries and other notables. The populace crowded into the rest of the hall, a dozen voices clamoring at once, each claiming that his cause should be the first heard. The more prudent litigants joined not the fray, but held whispered communications with the secretaries, passing bribes, euphemistically called fees, into the hands of one or another. When the greed of the underlings was satisfied, one of them would whisper to the *Kadi*, who would promptly call such and such a case. It seemed to be ordinarily taken for granted that judgment would go for the litigant who had bribed highest. But meantime a poor woman on the skirts of the crowd perpetually interrupted the proceedings with loud cries for justice. She was sternly bidden to be silent, and reproachfully told that she came there every day. "And so I will," she cried out, "till the *Kadi* hears me." At length, at the end of a suit, the judge impatiently demanded, "What does that woman want?" Her story was soon told. Her only son had been taken for a soldier, and she was alone, and could not till her

piece of ground; yet the tax-gatherer had forced her to pay the impost, from which as a lone widow she could be exempt. The judge asked a few questions, and said, "Let her be exempt." Thus her perseverance was rewarded. Had she had money to fee a clerk, she might have been excused long before.

Jesus' story has fewer details and only two characters but otherwise reflects a nearly identical setting. The judge finally yields to the plaintiff's pleas: "Even though I don't fear God or care about men, yet because this widow keeps bothering me, I will see that she gets justice, so that she won't eventually wear me out with her coming!" (The phrase "wear me out" actually translates a boxer's term for a repeated blow under the eye.)

Once again Jesus is presenting a parable of contrasts. In our prayers we may sometimes feel like the widow: alone, powerless, a victim of unfairness, disregarded, the least and last person in line. The truth, though, is the opposite. We have both an advocate and a direct line to a loving Father who has nothing in common with the insensitive judge in the story. When God seems slow to respond, we may suspect a lack of concern. Jesus corrects the misconception, pointing beyond how we may feel to an assurance of God's mercy. If even this widow gets justice from a heartless judge, how much more will "God bring about justice for his chosen ones, who cry out to him day and night?"

And then, just as the audience settles back in comfortable reassurance, comes the sting in the tail: "However, when the Son of Man comes, will he find faith on the earth?" The disciples would have known exactly what Jesus meant, for he had just been talking about his eventual return, the second coming. Justice will surely reign one day. Appearing this time in power and great glory, the Son of Man has pledged to turn the tables on this violent planet, righting every wrong and restoring the world to what God intended: a world without unjust judges and neglected widows; without any poverty, or death, suffering, or rebellion. Until that future day, some will be tempted to doubt, to disbelieve in God completely or to see God as a merciless judge.

Years after hearing this parable in person, the apostle Peter wrote that in the last days some will scoff at such prophecies: "Where is this 'coming' he promised? Ever since our fathers died, everything goes on as it has since the beginning of creation." And after twenty more centuries of waiting, the conditions of this unredeemed planet further tempt us to give up, to lose faith in a powerful, loving God. Jesus told the story of the nagging widow to teach us to "always pray and not give up." History is a test of faith, and the correct response to that test is persistent prayer.

Older versions of the Bible apply the little-used word "importunate" to the widow and the borrower in Jesus' stories. Sometimes our requests will seem annoying, as that word implies. I think of William Wilberforce submitting the same bill, year after year, before the British Parliament as he argued importunately for the abolition of slavery. Or of Senator William Proxmire giving a speech every day on the floor of the Senate—3211 speeches delivered over nineteen years—until his colleagues finally passed a bill outlawing genocide. I think of Sister Helen Prejean, portrayed in the movie *Dead Man Walking*, who tirelessly crosses the United States pleading against the death penalty. And of Martin Luther King Jr. as he addressed the bloodied Selma marchers from the steps of Alabama's state capitol, voicing again and again their question about justice: "How long? . . . How long? . . . How long will it take?"

Activists who take up a cause—third world debt, AIDS in Africa, homelessness, abortion, sexual trafficking, racism, hate crimes, drunk driving, health care, unjust wars, the environment, pornography, prison reform, terrorism, human rights, and a hundred others—will doubtless grow weary and may be tempted to give up the fight. To them, God must resemble the callous judge or the crotchety neighbor in Jesus' stories. Jesus insists otherwise. Unlike the judge and the neighbor, God has infinite tolerance for our requests and demands, especially those supporting the cause of God's own kingdom. Why else would the Bible include so many importuning psalms, so many prophetic laments?

In his sermon "The Parable of the Importunate Widow," Helmut Thielicke notes that "God is doing nothing less than offering to his praying church a part in his government of the world." The giants of history, Thielicke says (thinking of his contemporaries Hitler and Stalin), stride across the stage under the delusion that they are directing the drama of the world, whereas in reality they are only bit players permitted onstage for a moment. Real power rests in those who perceive history as God's own drama, who tap into a power accessible only to those who ask and seek and knock. Prayer sets God loose. As we revolt against the world's disorder in our actions and in our prayers, refusing to resign ourselves to evil, we demonstrate that there remains, in Jesus' phrase, "faith on the earth."

Generations may pass before persistent prayer receives its answer. How many soldiers died before Thielicke's own prayers for peace and justice in his homeland Germany were answered? How many Jews died praying for a future at a time when it seemed the entire race was being incinerated? Filipinos prayed importunately for relief before People Power brought down a corrupt regime. Millions languished in prison camps before the Iron Curtain fell to the ranks of peaceful protestors. How many Chinese Christians still suffer imprisonment and torture while outside the prison walls an unprecedented spiritual revival continues to gather steam?

On a more personal level, how many abuse victims plead for healing and still wake up every day feeling wounded and ashamed? Addicts pray for deliverance and then rise each day to fight the same relentless battles. Parents grieve in prayer over children who seem determined to live self-destructively.

I will always remember an alcoholic friend who expressed to me his frustration at praying daily for God to remove his desire for drink, only to find each morning his thoughts turning to Jack Daniel's whiskey. Was God even listening? Later, it dawned on him that the desire for alcohol was the main reason he prayed so diligently. Persistent temptation had compelled persistent prayer.

Evil looms like a great iron gate—"the gates of hell" in Jesus' image— and prayers hit against it like hammer strokes. Gates don't threaten or even advance. They just stand there, awaiting the onslaught. Our prayers may seem as tinny as the sound a hammer makes when it bounces off a sheet of metal, but we have Jesus' strong promise that the gates of hell will not prevail. They will surely fall, shattering into pieces like the Berlin Wall that once divided Germany, like the Iron Curtain that once divided Europe.

Once Is Not Enough

Author Jerry Sittser sees persistence through the eyes of a parent. "My kids have asked me for many things over the years—a CD player, bicycle, boat, car, house, exotic vacations . . . You name it, they have asked it. I ignore them most of the time. I am as hardhearted as they come, a parent made of granite. My ears perk up, however, when they persist, because persistence usually means they are serious about something."

Unlike a human parent, God knows my true motive, whether pure or impure, noble or selfish, from the moment of the original request. As I ponder Jesus' stories, I cannot help wondering why God places such a premium on persistence. If I find it tedious to repeat the same requests over and over, surely God tires of hearing them. Why must I pound on the door or elbow my way into the courtroom? Why won't a single heartfelt request suffice?

In search of clues, I turn first to the account of Jesus' life, and in several scenes I can see the value of persistence. After Lazarus died, his two sisters, the industrious Martha and meditative Mary, both accused Jesus: "Lord, if you had been here, my brother would not have died." They vented their accumulated grief and frustration, so much so that Jesus, too, sank into sorrow—before granting their deepest wish in one of his greatest miracles.

In another scene, a Canaanite woman pestered Jesus about her afflicted daughter. "Send her away, for she keeps crying out after us," urged the disciples, reminiscent of the hard-hearted villains in Jesus' parables. Even Jesus brushed her off, first ignoring her request and then challenging her right to make it. The foreign woman persisted and Jesus, impressed, granted her wish and then held her up as a model of faith.

Beside a well in Samaria, Jesus parried with a woman about her lifestyle and her religious beliefs. On the way to Jerusalem, he engaged a rich young man in a discussion on the dangers of wealth. The woman persisted and found her life transformed; the rich man gave up and turned away sad.

From these scenes I learn about God's interest in the process I go through. Always respectful of human freedom, God does not twist arms. God views my persistence as a sign of genuine desire for change, the one prerequisite for spiritual growth. When I really want something, I strive and persist. Whether it's climbing Colorado's mountains, chasing the woodpeckers away from my roof, or getting a high-speed Internet connection for my home, I'll do whatever it takes. Do I show the same spirit in prayer?

"Prayer does not change God, but it changes him who prays." Søren Kierkegaard may have first made that remark, but I have seen it repeated in a dozen books and articles. For reasons discussed in the previous chapter [not included in this excerpt] (mainly the Bible's own testimony), I cannot fully agree with the first half of the formula. God wants us to bring our requests boldly and without reservation. By failing to do so I will likely miss out on some delightful surprises. What if the ten with leprosy by the side of the road had not shouted out to Jesus for healing or if the Canaanite woman had shyly abandoned the request for her daughter?

All too often pray-ers use God's presumed changelessness as an excuse not to pray: "If God has already decided the future, why bother?" That very fatalism, ironically, defeats the second half of the formula, for we do indeed change in the very process of storming heaven with our prayers. If I stop believing that God listens to my requests—the emphatic point of Jesus' two parables—I will likely stop praying, thus closing off God's primary mode of relationship with me.

Persistent prayer keeps bringing God and me together, with several important benefits. As I pour out my soul to God, I get it off my chest, so to speak, unloading some of my burden to One who can handle it better. Little by little, as I get to know God I learn that God has nothing in common with an unjust judge or a stingy neighbor, though at times it may seem so. What I learn from spending time with God then better equips me to discern what God wants to do on earth, as well as my role in that plan.

Cicero gave a blunt assessment of the purpose of pagan prayer: "We do not pray to Jupiter to make us good, but to give us material benefits." For the Christian, something like the reverse applies. We may approach God with some material benefit in mind, and sometimes, blessedly, we receive it. But in the very act of praying we also open up a channel that God can use in transforming us, in making us good. Persistent prayer changes me by helping me see the world, and my life, through God's eyes. As the relationship progresses I realize that God has a clearer picture of what I need than I do.

When I persistently pursue another person, I am usually trying to persuade that person to adopt my point of view. I want the car salesman to match my price, the neighbor to vote for my candidate. I may, especially in the early stages of prayer, approach God the same way, but inevitably I find that God is the wise and senior partner in the relationship. I find, in fact, that God has been asking, seeking, knocking too, in the subtle ways I so easily ignore.

"A God that should fail to hear, receive, attend to one single prayer, the feeblest or worst, I cannot believe in; but a God that would grant every request of every man or every company of men, would be an evil God—that is no God, but a demon," said George MacDonald. Prayer is not a monologue but a true dialogue in which both parties accommodate to the other. Although I bring my honest concerns to God, over time I may come away with an entirely different set of concerns. When Peter went on a roof to pray (Acts 10), he was mainly thinking about food. Little did he know that he would descend from the roof convicted of racism and legalism. In persistent prayer, my own desires and plans gradually harmonize with God's.

Winning by Losing

"Why should I spend an hour in prayer when I do nothing during that time but think about people I am angry with, people who are angry with me, books I should read and books I should write, and thousands of other silly things that happen to grab my mind for a moment?" Henri Nouwen posed that question in different forms, toying with different answers. Sometimes he fell back on the need for spiritual discipline, for being faithful even with no apparent reward: "We must pray not first of all because it feels good or helps, but because God loves us and wants our attention."

In the end, Nouwen concluded that "sitting in the presence of God for one hour each morning—day after day, week after week, and month after month, in total confusion and with a myriad of distractions—radically changes my life." He learned humility and dependence, and after hours of persistent prayer with no obvious sign of fruitfulness, he realized that a small, gentle voice had indeed been speaking all the while.

"Prayer does not change God, but changes him who prays"? Perhaps, sometimes, the internal changes wrought through prayer make possible the answers that we have long been seeking—the "change" in God if you will. Persistent prayer leads us into a new spiritual state for God to deal with. Perhaps that is why Abraham, Moses, Jacob, and the others found themselves wrestling so fiercely: the apparent struggle against God was developing in them the Godlike qualities that God wanted all along.

"Isn't it the greatest possible disaster, when you are wrestling with God, not to be beaten?" asked Simone Weil. To put it another way, what feels like a defeat at the time may emerge as an enduring victory. Jacob the cheat walked cockily on two good legs; Israel limped into history as the father of nations. The real value of persistent prayer is not so much that we get what we want as that we become the person we should be.

Whether climbing a mountain or writing a book, I have a goal-oriented, accomplish-the-mission attitude toward life, and prayer stops me in my tracks. I learn that I cannot "fix" the people I am praying for.

I cannot get everything I want in the time frame I want. I must slow down and wait. I have to present my requests in a manner that seems at first like surrender. I "give them up" to God, and through that act of submission God can at last begin to grow in me the qualities, or "fruit," that I needed all along: peace, patience, kindness, goodness, faithfulness, gentleness, self-control.

A person prays, said Augustine, "that he himself may be constructed, not that God may be instructed." I examine my own erratic prayer life and see it as a time when God has indeed worked to lop off the protuberances and smooth the rough edges. I see defeats and victories both. Like a child who quits badgering a parent, I have sometimes found that I get an answer to my persistent request after I have learned to do without it. The answer then comes as a surprise, an unexpected gift of grace. I seek the gift, find instead the Giver, and eventually come away with the gift I no longer seek.

Luke's version of the parable of the crotchety neighbor ends with these words: "If you then, though you are evil, know how to give good gifts to your children, how much more will your Father in heaven give the *Holy Spirit* to those who ask him!" Matthew repeats the same saying, with one change: "If you, then, though you are evil, know how to give good gifts to your children, how much more will your Father in heaven give *good gifts* to those who ask him!"

In prayer we present requests, sometimes repeatedly, and then put ourselves in a state to receive the result. We pray for what God wants to give us, which may turn out to be good gifts or it may be the Holy Spirit. (From God's viewpoint there is no better response to persistent prayer than the gift of the Holy Spirit, God's own self.) Like Peter, we may pray for food and get a lesson in racism; like Paul we may pray for healing and get humility. We may ask for relief from trials and instead get patience to bear them. We may pray for release from prison and instead get strength to redeem the time while there. Asking, seeking, and knocking does have an effect on God, as Jesus insists, but it also has a lasting effect on the asker-seeker-knocker.

WHY PRAY?

"For we are God's workmanship, created in Christ Jesus to do good works," Paul wrote the Ephesians. *Workmanship* conveys rather clumsily the meaning of the Greek word *poiema*, origin of the English word *poem*. We are God's work of art, Paul is saying. Of all people, Paul with his history of beatings, prison, shipwreck, and riots, knew the travail involved in the fashioning of that art—and the role that prayer played. Prayer offers an opportunity for God to remodel us, to chisel marble like a sculptor, touch up colors like an artist, edit words like a writer. The work continues until death, never perfected in this life.

∼ Yearning for Fluency

The paradox of prayer is that it asks for a serious effort while it can only be received as a gift. We cannot plan, organize or manipulate God; but without a careful discipline, we cannot receive him either.

— HENRI NOUWEN

I CANNOT REMEMBER A TIME without prayer. As a child I recited prayers before falling asleep and bowed my head before every meal. I faithfully attended Wednesday night prayer meetings and New Year's Eve watch night services, both of which sorely taxed a child's ability to stay awake. I prayed with childlike trust, so much so that friends of the family who lost a wedding ring or a family pet would phone to ask for my prayers, often calling back later to report a happy result. (Meanwhile my own family pets would get run over, die of distemper, or get attacked by neighbors' dogs despite my pleas for their protection.)

For several years I attended a Bible college that enforced praying with the rigor of a military academy. A bell rang at 6:00 a.m. and by 6:30 every student was required to begin a half-hour "quiet time" of Bible reading and prayer. Deans sometimes made surprise checks in the dorms, and stories abounded of a dean opening a door and switching on a light to find one student kneeling by the side of his bed while his roommate sat on the bed with an open Bible, both sound asleep in total darkness.

The school also scheduled periodic "prayer days." Instead of going to classes we prayed privately and in groups most of the day until gathering for a triumphant service of prayer and testimony in the evening. Students reported on answers to prayer, such as the timely financial gifts that allowed them to stay in school. At one of these services I heard my roommate tearfully confess a series of wild escapades that I knew he was embellishing. Like prisoners bragging about their crimes, young sinners gained inverted prestige through dramatic public repentance. Another student asked prayer for his girlfriend, critically injured in an auto accident while driving to see him. This sad, lonely boy from my hometown in fact had no girlfriend, was gay, and would eventually die of AIDS; he had made up the story to attract attention and sympathy.

In the years since, while working with Christian organizations and serving on various church committees, I have sat through many group prayer sessions. Some moved me deeply and bonded the group together. Others seemed an exercise in positioning, and I too felt the temptation to gain status by praying impressively, my words addressed as much to those around me as to God.

I have experienced times when prayer made little sense. Questions I have already mentioned (Why tell God what God already knows? Why ask God to be merciful if God is by nature merciful? Why pray at all?) muzzled me. For a solid year I could come up with no authentic prayers of my own and simply read from prayers in a *Liturgy of the Hours*, asking God to take those written words and accept them as my prayers whether I felt them sincerely or not. Then one day the cloud lifted and I wondered what had been my problem all that time.

I have not since experienced such a time of blockage or desolation, yet I have never stopped struggling with the act of prayer. When I hear of people who spend an hour a day meditating, I wonder how they do it. I strain to spend fifteen minutes, and anything longer tends to degenerate into distraction and lapses of concentration. Typically, I have the sense that my cluttered world of tasks undone and letters unanswered imposes on an ordered time with God. I am learning, though, to dismantle the barriers separating the act of prayer from the rest of life and instead to invite God to "impose" on my tightly ordered life.

Adjusting Expectations

Even when prayer seems a duty, like a homework assignment, we sustain the hope that it could grow into something more. A hidden treasure lies inside, if only we can quarry it. A new country awaits us, if only we can find the language in which to converse. We babble like infants, yearning for fluency. "I was less a man praying than a man *being* a man praying," recalls Frederick Buechner about a phase when his prayers seemed self-conscious and stagy.

Some who attempt prayer never have the sense of anyone listening on the other end. They blame themselves for doing it wrong, feeling ever a failure. An Australian wrote me about his concern for those who feel *autistic* in prayer: not only the depressed and those with borderline personality disorders, but also ordinary, timid people in the pews who feel undeserving of God's attention.

Another friend of mine who knew I was investigating prayer wrote that in her experience few people find prayer fulfilling, easy, or rewarding. She added,

I think prayer is analogous to sex. (People's ears always perk up when I say that.) Most people would complain about their sex lives; a few do really well. Sex and prayer are intimate and over-glamorized relationships. We all are led to believe that we should be in the stratosphere in sex and in prayer. It sets up a false expectation. And breaks down intimacy.

This woman spent several months in Africa, which forced her to adopt to a slower pace. There she found the silence to pray in a new way. "Again, similar to sex, when we are so busy and filled with the cacophony of life, it is hard to relax, be quiet and communicate."

As I thought about her unlikely analogy, it occurred to me that reading a book about prayer has some parallels to reading a sex manual. What sounds so thrilling on paper bears little resemblance to how sex usually plays out between two vulnerable people who approach it with very different expectations. Like sex, prayer centers in relationship more than in technique, and the differences between the two parties in prayer are far more profound than the differences between two lovers. Should it surprise us that problems arise?

A media-saturated culture conditions us to expect a quick fix to every problem. Relationship problems, however, rarely lend themselves to quick and easy solutions. I have not seen, for instance, that shelves of books on "how to save your marriage" have had any discernible effect on divorce rates. If relating to another person proves so resistant to formulaic advice, how much more does relating to God? The secret to keeping company with God will likely not be found in a new set of tapes, another book, a different preacher, a weekend seminar.

After reading scores of books and interviewing scores of people about prayer, I would expect a more noticeable improvement in my own prayer life. If I invested the same energy in, say, golf or learning a foreign language, I would likely see results. Still I find that prayer involves an effort of will. Sometimes it proves rewarding, sometimes not, at least not in ways I can detect at the time. Prayer requires the faith to believe that God listens, though I have no hard evidence, and that my prayers matter. Neither belief comes easily to me.

When I enter another culture, I have to communicate by their rules, not mine. In South India I learned that shaking the head from side to side means yes, not no. When I got married, I learned that men are from Mars and women are from Venus; after thirty-five years I am still discovering ways in which we differ. And when I seek to know God, I must learn a new way of communicating. I am seeking company with an invisible God, after all.

I recently heard from a missionary doctor who has spent the past three years in Ecuador. His letter recounted some of the frustrations involved in learning a language. Even after three years he makes childish mistakes in grammar, looks foolish in front of the native-speakers, and can express only haltingly what his brain processes fluently. Speaking Spanish has been a continuing lesson in humility, he said. He makes progress, yes, but every day he realizes that he has failed to communicate fully and has missed nuances of meaning.

Reading his letter, I drew the parallel to prayer. If I want fluency in a foreign language, I must set aside time, no doubt giving up something else in the process. I must keep working at it, persisting despite the awkward feelings of a beginner. I persevere only because I value the final result. Nearly everything worthwhile—learning a sport, mastering the guitar, improving computer skills—involves the same process.

Prayer remains a struggle for me. On the other hand, so does forgiving someone who has wronged me. So does loving my neighbor. So does caring for the needy. I persist because I am fulfilling God's command, and also because I believe I am doing what is best for me whether or not I feel like it at the time. Moreover, I believe that my perseverance, in some unfathomable way, brings pleasure to God. We should always pray and not give up, Jesus taught.

I take dark encouragement in the fact that after following Jesus around for months, the disciples still had no clue and had to ask, "Teach us to pray." I take encouragement from Christians far advanced in spiritual disciplines who have similar struggles. (If you doubt that, read some accounts of Trappist monks, who spend all day pursuing life with God and who confront the same obstacles that stump us part-timers.) How do we learn to pray? Mother Teresa answers, "By praying. . . . If you want to pray better, you must pray more."

The great English preacher Leslie Weatherhead's experience echoes that of many others:

I have always found prayer difficult. So often it seems like a fruitless game of hide and seek in which we seek and God hides. I know God is very patient with me. Without that patience I should be lost. But frankly I have to be patient with him. With no other friend would I go on seeking with such scant, conscious response. Yet I cannot leave prayer alone for long. My need drives me to him. And I have a feeling that he has his own reasons for hiding himself, and that finally my seeking will prove infinitely worthwhile. . . . I long for more satisfaction, but I cannot cease from questing. Jesus sometimes found prayer difficult. Some of his most agonized prayers were not answered. But he did not give up his praying. I frankly have little to show for all my prayers, but I cannot give up, for "my soul longeth for God," and I know that outside God there is nothing at all but death.

Choosing a Routine

In the midst of a hectic, confusing period of his life, Henri Nouwen took a sabbatical from his professorship at Yale and spent seven months at a Trappist monastery in upstate New York. He asked a mentor there for advice on how to develop a deeper prayer life in the midst of his busyness. When he tried to pray, he said, his mind drifted to the many things he had to do, most of which seemed more urgent and important than prayer. The mentor recommended that Nouwen set a prayer schedule that he would stick to at all costs. He suggested an hour in the morning before work and a half hour before going to bed, a schedule far more lenient than the monks' own.

Nouwen decided on a more realistic prayer regimen of half an hour each day. At first his thoughts ran wild, like untamed animals. He kept at it, telling himself, "Since I am here for this half hour anyhow, I might just as well pray." The sense of awkwardness gradually faded, and in time he felt his soul settling down to a more calming rhythm. It may seem that nothing happens when you pray, he observed. But when you stay with a routine, over time you realize that something indeed has happened.

Along with Nouwen, I too appreciate prayer mostly in retrospect. The process itself feels like work. I look for ways to avoid it and keep glancing at the clock as I'm praying. During the day, however, thoughts and impressions come to mind that stem directly from my prayers. I am far more likely to view events that occur and people I encounter from

God's point of view. Like a lingering scent, prayer carries over into the rest of the day.

I must admit that when I read the masters of prayer I feel myself tensing against their advice to make prayer a discipline. Mother Teresa prescribed a full hour of contemplation for each of the sisters in her order. (They rise at 4:30 a.m. and take a cold-water bath before morning prayers.) Some medieval authors recommended pausing before every prayer to tell yourself you might die at the end of your prayer, in order to focus its intensity. When I read such advice, I have an allergic reaction that probably traces back to that six o'clock bell in the Bible college.

Yet I remind myself that in some areas I willingly show discipline, somehow finding time for what matters to me. I check email without fail. I exercise faithfully. I keep doctor's appointments. I sit at my desk and work whether I feel in the mood or not. And if I travel away from my wife, I think about her during the day and call her in the evening.

Don Postema says, "I used to write in my daily calendar '7 – 7:30 a.m.: Prayer.' But many times I passed that up. It was one more thing to pass by that day. Now I write '7 – 7:30 a.m.: God.' Somehow that's a little harder to neglect." I have found that my reluctance to pray increases when I regard it as a necessary discipline and decreases when I see it as a time to keep company with God.

True prayer comes from within, from the longing of the heart. A woman named Judy Morford expressed this well:

> My own prayer life has been through many changes over the years. As a young mother, I had a five-year-old, a three-year-old, and a one-year-old, and I found the only time I could really pray was literally in the middle of the night. If I woke up then, I would pray. As the kids grew older, I began to get up at 4:30 in the morning to pray. I still don't have ideal conditions for regular prayer. As a mother of three teenagers and working full time, I sometimes get too tired to pray. But most days I'm able to work in some time for quiet prayer.

> Because of my changing schedule over the years, I've asked myself, *Just what does God expect of me in my prayer life?* The answer I come up with is he wants a love relationship. He doesn't want a hired servant; he wants a bride. A true love will always find a way. It may not always be the same way, or the prescribed way, but it will be a way that reflects love. That's what God wants from me.

The routine of prayer for Judy Morford bears little resemblance to that of Henri Nouwen, not to mention his Trappist adviser. I must find my own way to pray, not someone else's. And as life changes, my prayer practice will no doubt change with it. A person battling chronic illness will pray differently than a college student who mainly worries about final exams and a noisy roommate. Taking a mission trip, getting married, managing a houseful of kids, giving care to an aging parent—every major life change will have its effect on prayer, both its practice and its content. The only fatal mistake is to stop praying and not begin again.

Showing Up

Life today conspires against a regular, satisfying prayer time. Reading the classic devotional literature, I am struck by how much of it came from the pens of people who lived in communities organized for that purpose (such as convents and monasteries) or from those who had servants to handle the time-consuming chores (they say nothing of the servants' prayer lives). I find scant advice on prayer written by a mother of three teenagers or an executive who puts in seventy-hour weeks at the office.

Add to modern hindrances the barrage of "noise" in an information society—chat rooms, mobile phones, television, text messaging, iPods, BlackBerry Internet devices—and prayer simply gets drowned out. In airports I see business people walking around with Bluetooth earpieces permanently attached to their ears, waiting for the next interruption. Of course, all the electronic devices have an on/off switch, but somehow their offerings seem more productive or enticing than sitting quietly in conversation with God.

Let's be honest: by most standards they *are* more productive and enticing than prayer. Some manuals on prayer imply that time spent with God will rank as the high point of a day and that prayer flowing spontaneously from anointed lips will usher in miraculous answers. Instead, the pray-er finds herself battling boredom, fatigue, and a nagging feeling that she's wasting time. *What went wrong?* she wonders.

Daniel Yankelovich, an astute observer of social trends, points to a cultural shift that occurred in the West in the 1970s. Before then, society valued self-denial or "deferred gratification." Spouses sacrificed, even if it meant holding two jobs and accepting transfers to other cities, in pursuit of long-term goals. Parents trapped in an unsatisfying marriage stayed together for the sake of the children. In the 1970s the rules changed: the self-denial ethic morphed into a self-fulfillment ethic. We listen to our emotional needs and want them fulfilled now, without sacrifice, without waiting. We buy whatever we want on credit and jettison anything that proves complicated or irksome (like a troublesome marriage, for instance).

Under the new rules prayer loses out. It requires discipline, involves persevering through periods of darkness and dryness, and its results are difficult to measure. Rarely does it satisfy emotional cravings right away.

Indeed, the New Testament presents prayer as a weapon in a prolonged struggle. Jesus' parables on prayer show a widow pestering a judge and a man pounding on his neighbor's door. After painting a picture of the Christian as a soldier outfitted with the "full armor of God," Paul gives four direct commands to pray. Elsewhere, Paul urges his protégé Timothy to endure hardship like a soldier, to toil like a farmer, to compete like an athlete.

I have neither farmed nor served in the military but for thirty years I have been a runner, often entering charity races. I remember well how it all started. I met a young man named Peter Jenkins at a writers' conference as he was working on the book A *Walk Across America*, which later became a national bestseller. As he recounted some of his adventures on a long walk across the country, he said, "I get tired of these reporters flying down from New York, renting a car, then driving out to meet me. They hit the electric window button of their air-conditioned car, lean out, and ask, 'So, Peter, what's it like to walk across America?' I'd like a reporter to walk with me for a while!" Without thinking, I volunteered.

As our agreed-upon time approached, I realized that if I planned to walk through Texas in July with a sixty-pound pack on my back, I had better get into shape. I bought some cheap running shoes, stepped out the door, and sprinted down the driveway, expecting to run a few miles. At the end of the block I pulled up, gasping and wheezing, with an abrupt lesson in physical fitness. Lay off exercise for a decade or more, and the body no longer responds.

I ran as far as I could that day—one block—then walked a block, ran another block, and limped home humiliated. The next day I ran two blocks, kept walking, and ran some more. Within six weeks, just in time for my Texas assignment, I was running seven miles without stopping. That began a routine of aerobic exercise that continues to this day. My body has become so accustomed to the regimen that if I have to skip a few days because of injury or illness I feel edgy and restless.

I learned early on never to ask myself, "Do you feel like running today?" I just do it. Why? I can think of many reasons. Regular exercise allows me to eat what I want without worrying about weight gain. It does long-term good for my heart and lungs. It allows me to do other activities, such as skiing and mountain climbing. All these benefits represent the kind of "deferred gratification" Daniel Yankelovich referred to.

As with physical exercise, much of the benefit of prayer comes as a result of consistency, the simple act of showing up. The writer Nancy Mairs says she attends church in the same spirit in which a writer goes to her desk every morning, so that if an idea comes along she'll be there to receive it. I approach prayer the same way. Many days I would be hard-pressed to describe a direct benefit. I keep on, though, whether it feels like I am profiting or not. I show up in hopes of getting to know God better, and perhaps hearing from God in ways accessible only through quiet and solitude.

For years I resisted a regular routine of prayer, believing that communication with God should be spontaneous and free. As a result I prayed infrequently and with little satisfaction. Eventually I learned that spontaneity often flows from discipline. Leonardo da Vinci spent ten years drawing ears, elbows, hands, and other parts of the body in many different aspects. Then one day he set aside the exercises and painted what he saw. Likewise, athletes and musicians never become great without regular practice. I found that I needed the discipline of regularity to make possible those exceptional times of free communication with God.

The English word *meditate* derives from a Latin word which means "to rehearse." Virgil speaks of a shepherd boy "meditating" on his flute. Often my prayers seem like a kind of rehearsal. I go over basic notes (the Lord's Prayer), practice familiar pieces (the Psalms), and try out a few new tunes. Mainly, I show up.

Two Worlds

In medieval times, and still today in monasteries, the chiming of a church bell would cause all who heard it to stop and say the prescribed prayer. It forced them to remember God. Living in a place where church bells do not ring, I must make a deliberate effort to remember. Otherwise my mind fills with different content: images from the television screen, details of pending trips, a pile of laundry, anxiety over a sick friend.

When I pray, it may seem that I am narrowing my world, retreating from the real world into a prayer closet in Jesus' metaphor. Actually I am entering another world, just as real but invisible, a world that has power to change both me and the world I seem to be retreating from. Regular prayer helps me to protect inner space, to prevent the outer world from taking over. "Blessed are the pure in heart, for they will see

God," Jesus said. When I think of how long a single image crafted by Hollywood lust-masters can live on in my mind, I understand his saying. So often I fill my mind with images that crowd out all room for God. Prayer involves a "renewing of the mind," a two-stage process of purging out what displeases God and damages me (the same, it turns out) and allowing God to fill my mind with what matters far more.

Contact with God doesn't just provide a moment of spiritual ecstasy; it equips me for the rest of life. I corral a few minutes of calm in the morning in hopes that I can carry some part of that calm into the rest of the day. If I pray consistently I feel free and strong, able to meet the challenges and temptations of the day. As the Psalms demonstrate so well, prayer does not mean retreating away from life, but rather bringing the stuff of our world—the rhythms of nature, harassing problems, disturbed emotions, personality conflicts—before God, then asking for a new perspective and new energy to take back to that world.

In short, prayer invites God into my world, and ushers me into God's. Jesus himself, who spent many hours in solitary prayer, invariably returned to a busy world of weddings, dinners, and crowds of sick and needy people. He rejected Peter's suggestion to build a tent on a mountaintop and returned instead to the masses below. Following that pattern, I look for ways to bring the two worlds together, God's and mine, to let them become one.

The morning offers a chance to plot out the day in advance, to bring before God every scheduled appointment and phone call as well as to ask God to keep me mindful of any sacred interruptions. None of us knows what any day will bring, of course, and I find it helps to request in advance a sensitivity to whatever might transpire. I need to tune in to God's work behind the scenes. As my pastor in Chicago used to pray, "God, show me what you are doing today, and how I can be a part of it." Amazingly, when I preview my day in prayer, priorities will tend to rearrange themselves during the course of the day. An unexpected phone call may take on more significance than the scheduled task of finishing my income tax forms.

On the other hand, prayer in the evening provides a natural coda to the day. I can review all that happened, reflect on what I learned, repent of how I failed, and deliver into God's hands all that remains unresolved and troubling. Many times I go to bed confused about a computer error or some problem in my writing and awake the next day with a fresh idea on how to solve it. Regardless, if I do not schedule such times in the morning or evening, they do not happen of their own accord. I have to make time, just as I make time for physical exercise, for watching the news, for eating.

Like many people, I have found that a regular place helps settle me into a spirit of prayer. President Jimmy Carter reserved a room next to the Oval Office as a private place to pray. I know a woman who has constructed a "prayer closet" in her oversized bathroom. She hangs artwork in that corner, lights candles, and retreats there several times a day for the sole purpose of prayer.

When he was on the faculty at Yale, Henri Nouwen converted a walk-in clothes closet into a prayer closet. "The simple fact that I'm in the closet means I'm praying," he said. "I might have a thousand things to think about while I'm in there, but the fact that I'm sitting in this physical place means I'm praying. I force myself to stay there for fifteen minutes. I do my best to center my mind and clear it of distracting thoughts and get down to prayer, but if after fifteen minutes I haven't been entirely successful, I say, 'Lord this was my prayer, even all this confusion. Now I'm going back to the world.'"

I begin each day in a solarium that looks out over a copse of trees. Early rising birds flit to the birdfeeder and heated birdbath. Squirrels stretch themselves awake and scurry down to the spilled birdseed. The first rays of sun shoot over the surrounding hills. I have the sense that God has already been at work that day and through the night, and my own petty problems take on a different light in the rhythms of the larger world, and of eternity.

Ben Patterson, currently chaplain at Westmont College, California, tells of a time when he ruptured a disc and the doctor prescribed six weeks of total bed rest. Heavily medicated and lying flat on his back, he found that reading was virtually impossible. In that incapacitated state, he learned an important lesson about prayer.

I was helpless.

I was also terrified. What was this all going to mean? How was I to take care of my family? What about the church? I was the only pastor it had, and I could do nothing for it. Out of sheer desperation I decided to pray for the church. I opened the church directory and prayed for each member of the congregation, daily. It took nearly two hours, but since there was nothing else I could do for the church, I figured I might as well pray for it. It was not piety that made me do it, it was boredom and frustration. But over the weeks the prayer times grew sweet. One day near the end of my convalescence, I was praying and I told the Lord, "You know, it's been wonderful, these prolonged times we've spent together. It's too bad I don't have time to do this when I'm well."

God's answer came swift and blunt. He said to me, "Ben, you have just as much time when you're well as when you're sick. It's the same twenty-four hours in either case. The trouble with you is that when you're well, you think you're in charge. When you're sick, you know you're not."

∿ Unanswered Prayer: Living with the Mystery

O that thou shouldst give dust a tongue
To crie to thee
And then not heare it crying!

— GEORGE HERBERT

SOME, BUT NOT ALL, unanswered prayers trace back to a fault in the one who prays. Some, but not all, trace back to God's mystifying respect for human freedom and refusal to coerce. Some, but not all, trace back to dark powers contending against God's rule. Some, but not all, trace back to a planet marred with disease, violence, and the potential for tragic accident. How, then, can we make sense of any single experience of unanswered prayer?

I take odd comfort in the fact that the Bible itself includes numerous prayers that went unanswered. Although we can only speculate why God does not answer a given prayer, these biblical examples lay down useful clues.

- After leading the Israelites through the wilderness for forty years, Moses pled with God to allow him to accompany them across the Jordan River before he died. God refused this request as punishment for Moses' past outbursts, which so rankled Moses that four times in his speeches to the Israelites in Deuteronomy he lashed out, blaming them for God's refusal. On other occasions Moses had talked God into "changing his mind." Not this time.

- King David spent a week, prostrate and spurning all food, praying that his infant son not die. As a consequence of his grievous sin, that prayer went unanswered: David and Bathsheba lost the child. Nevertheless, their next union led to the birth of Solomon, who would rule over Israel's Golden Age.

- Four characters in the Old Testament—Moses, Job, Jonah, and Elijah—actually prayed to die. Fortunately for them, God ignored their requests.

- Several times the armies of Israel prayed for victory over their enemies, only to suffer humiliating defeats. Each event prompted soul-searching. Did the army act precipitously, against God's orders? Had some soldier committed a war crime that displeased God?

- The prophet Habbakuk prayed for deliverance from the Babylonians; Jeremiah prayed that Jerusalem not be destroyed. Both prophets' prayers went unanswered, and each struggled to explain the reason to a defeated nation. "You have covered yourself with a cloud so that no prayer can get through," lamented the prophet in a book aptly titled Lamentations.

I have mentioned some of the twelve disciples' inappropriate prayers, such as calling for fire from heaven against a town. In one instance the disciples proved unable to perform a miracle of healing and seemed puzzled by the failure (see Matthew 17 and Mark 9). Jesus used the opportunity to rebuke their lack of faith. Although the disciples' prayers had gone unanswered, clearly it was God's will that the boy be healed, for Jesus then accomplished what they could not.

The apostle Paul had his share of unanswered prayers: you need only read his luminous prayers for churches and then read the sad record of those churches to realize how far short they fell of the ideal for which he prayed. In his most famous unanswered prayer, Paul pleaded with the

Lord three times for the removal of the "thorn in my flesh." In a model response to a negative answer, he put behind him the disappointment of not getting what he wanted and instead accepted what he got:

> Therefore I will boast all the more gladly about my weaknesses, so that Christ's power may rest on me. That is why, for Christ's sake, I delight in weaknesses, in insults, in hardships, in persecutions, in difficulties. For when I am weak, then I am strong.

Not even Jesus was exempt from unanswered prayer. In Gethsemane Jesus prayed with both the faith of protest and the faith of acquiescence. He turned for help first to God, pleading "let this cup pass"; then to his friends, who were sound asleep; then to the religious rulers, who accused him; then to the state, which sentenced him; then to the people, who rejected him. Finally he uttered that awful cry of dereliction, "My God, why have you forsaken me?" For C. S. Lewis, that sequence of helplessness illustrates "the human situation writ large. . . . Every rope breaks when you seize it. Every door is slammed shut as you reach it."

From these unanswered prayers I gain a glimmer of insight into the riddle of prayer. What if David's son had lived and reigned as king instead of Solomon? What if the prophets' prayers had been answered and Israel had established itself as a world power, its citizens holding their religion tight to their chests, unshared with the world? What if Paul had been healed, making him a more agile missionary perhaps but one of insufferable pride as he feared? Finally, what if Jesus had received the answer he prayed for in a moment of dread? His rescue would have meant the planet's ruin.

C. S. Lewis observes:

> The essence of request, as distinct from compulsion, is that it may or may not be granted. And if an infinitely wise Being listens to the requests of finite and foolish creatures, of course He will sometimes grant and sometimes refuse them. Invariable "success" in prayer would not prove the Christian doctrine at all. It would prove something much more like magic.

It is not unreasonable for a headmaster to say, "Such and such things you may do according to the fixed rules of this school. But such and such other things are too dangerous to be left to general rules. If you want to do them you must come and make a request and talk over the whole matter with me in my study. And then—we'll see."

Sweeping Promises

As Lewis acknowledged, the real problem lies not in the fact of refusal but in the Bible's lavish promises. In a nutshell, the main difficulty with unanswered prayers is that Jesus seemed to promise there need not be any.

Jesus could have said something like this: "I am bestowing the gift of prayer. You must realize, of course, that humans cannot have perfect wisdom, so there are limits as to whether your prayers will be answered. Prayer operates like a suggestion box. Spell out your requests clearly to God, and I guarantee that all requests will be carefully considered." That kind of statement about prayer I can easily live with. Instead, here is what Jesus said:

> I tell you the truth, if you have faith and do not doubt . . . you can say to this mountain, "Go, throw yourself into the sea," and it will be done. If you believe, you will receive whatever you ask for in prayer.

> Again, I tell you that if two of you on earth agree about anything you ask for, it will be done for you by my Father in heaven.

> Therefore I tell you, whatever you ask for in prayer, believe that you have received it, and it will be yours.

> You may ask me for anything in my name and I will do it.

These represent just a sampling of the New Testament's sweeping claims made in plain language. Some preachers seize on these passages as a kind of club, flogging the church for not taking them literally and faulting believers for having too little faith. But how to account for the unanswered prayers of Jesus and Paul? And how can we reconcile the lavish promises with the actual experience of so many sincere Christians who struggle with unanswered prayer?

One possible explanation centers in the specific group of people to whom Jesus was talking: the disciples. Could it be that Jesus gave the Twelve, handpicked to carry on the work after his death, certain rights and privileges in prayer that would not be normative for every follower? The Gospel writers do not explicitly say "These commands apply to the disciples only," but they do specify in each case that Jesus was speaking to his intimate disciples, not a large crowd.

Jesus invested in the disciples a unique discernment into God's will. "Everything that I learned from my Father I have made known to you," he told them at the Last Supper. After spending three years schooled directly by Jesus, they would presumably have a good idea of which prayers would further God's purpose on earth and which would be capricious or self-serving. (Yet the letters credited to Peter and John show that prayer did not operate like magic for the disciples either. Those two, like Paul, expressed frustration over developments in the church contrary to their prayers. And historians tell of the martyrdom of ten of the disciples. Surely the prayer "let this cup pass" must have run through their minds at some point.)

Another explanation focuses on the "fine print" that modifies the lavish promises. Virtually all of them contain a qualifier, such as "whatever you ask *in my name*," or "*If* you remain in me and my words remain in you." The assurance of answered prayers, still sweeping in its scope, comes with conditions. Am I abiding in Christ? Am I making requests according to his will? Am I obeying his commands? Each of these underscores the relationship, the companionship with God. The more we know God, the more we know God's will, the more likely our prayers will align with that will.

After pondering this problem for years and discussing it with "about every Christian I know, learned or simple, lay or clerical, within my own Communion or without," C. S. Lewis finally concluded that the kind of dauntless faith called for by Jesus "occurs only when the one who prays does so as God's fellow-worker, demanding what is needed for the joint work. It is the prophet's, the apostle's, the missionary's, the healer's prayer that is made with this confidence. . . . Something of the divine foreknowledge enters his mind." In other words, one who works in close partnership with God grows in the ability to discern what God wants to accomplish on earth, and prays accordingly.

A Time to Wait

In no way do I mean to dilute the majestic promises about prayer given by Jesus, James, John, and others in the New Testament. God knows— truly, God knows—I need more of the bold and simple faith those passages call for. On the other hand, considering them in isolation leads to a "name it and claim it" mentality that ignores much other revelation. The same Jesus who spoke of faith as a mustard seed also gave us the story about a widow wearing down a judge with her persistence. And all through the Bible spiritual giants wrestle with God in their prayers.

As we have seen, Jesus himself set limits to the requests he made. "Take this cup," he asked, and then added the modifier about the Father's will. He prayed that Peter's faith would hold firm, but not that Peter avoid all testing. He declined to pray for angels' help in rescuing him from execution.

So, too, do we all set limits to our prayers. Some things we can ask for unconditionally, such as forgiveness, and compassion for the poor, and progress in growing the fruit of the Spirit. Other requests are conditional, such as Paul's plea for relief from the "thorn." Some we refrain from asking out of respect for the natural laws that govern the planet. I pray that God will help my uncle cope with diabetes, but not that God restore his amputated leg. Nor do I pray that God would shift the orbit of planet Earth to counteract global warming. Instead, I ask what my own role should be in helping my uncle and in addressing environmental concerns.

I also learn, as I ponder the mystery of unanswered prayer, simply to wait.

The Lord is good unto them that wait for him. . .

But they that wait upon the Lord shall renew their strength; they shall mount up with wings as eagles; they shall run, and not be weary; and they shall walk, and not faint.

And let us not be weary in well doing: for in due season we shall reap, if we faint not.

Daniel waited three weeks for an answer to his prayer. Seeking guidance in the midst of war, Jeremiah waited ten days before receiving an answer. After climbing Mount Sinai to receive the Ten Commandments, Moses waited six days before hearing God's voice. Jesus, too, waited. When he performed an impressive miracle, his followers wanted to spread the word immediately. Jesus hushed them: "My time has not yet come." He understood something about God that we impatient types overlook: God acts *slowly*.

Think of the centuries that passed between the disruption caused by Adam and the reconciliation brought by Jesus: centuries that included Abraham's waiting for a child, the Israelites' waiting for liberation, the prophets' waiting for Messiah. Biblical history tells a meandering, zigzag tale of fits and starts, doglegs and detours. God's plan builds like a leisurely opera, not a Top 40 tune. For those of us caught in any one phrase of the opera, especially a mournful phrase, the music may seem unbearably sad. Onward it moves, at deliberate speed and with great effort.

The very tedium, the act of waiting itself, works to nourish in us qualities of patience, persistence, trust, gentleness, compassion—or it may do so, if we place ourselves in the stream of God's movement on earth. It may take more faith to trust God when we do not get what we ask for than when we do. Is that not the point of Hebrews 11? That chapter includes the poignant comment that the heroes of faith were "commended for their faith, yet none of them received what had been promised." It then intertwines their frustrated destiny with ours: "God had planned something better for us so that only together with us would they be made perfect." Faith calls us to trust in a future-oriented God.

Scoffers will call such a pledge into question, as the Bible freely admits. "They will say, '. . . Ever since our fathers died, everything goes on as it has since the beginning of creation.' . . . But do not forget this one thing, dear friends: With the Lord a day is like a thousand years, and a thousand years are like a day. The Lord is not slow in keeping his promise, as some understand slowness. He is patient with you, not wanting anyone to perish, but everyone to come to repentance." With all the time in the world, God waits, tolerating the insults of human history out of mercy, not impotence.

Even Psalms, the Bible's prayer book so profuse with groans and laments, circles back repeatedly to the theme of God's faithfulness. No matter how circumstances appear at any given moment, we can trust the fact that God still rules the universe. The divine reputation rests on a solemn pact that one day all shall be well.

The Surprise Factor

I have a friend in Japan who provides resources to the underground church in China and often worships among them. One day I asked her, "How do Chinese Christians pray? Do their prayers differ from what you hear in the U.S. or Japan?" She replied that the prayers closely follow the pattern of the Lord's Prayer. The church has spread most widely among the lower classes, and when they ask for daily bread and deliverance from evil, they mean it literally.

She continued, "I've heard Chinese Christians pray for the leaders of their government, but never for a change in the government—even in areas that persecute the unregistered churches. They pray very practically, thanking God for today's grace, asking for tomorrow's protection. They tell us visitors, 'Don't pray for me to get out of prison, please pray for courage and strength so that I can witness boldly in the prison and not lose faith.'"

When I visit places like Nepal and China, I come upon a paradox of answered and unanswered prayers. On the one hand, I hear remarkable stories of miracles. For example, the first Nepalese became a Christian in 1950. Now the church numbers more than half a million, and Nepalese church leaders estimate that 80 percent of the converts have resulted from physical healings: a Christian prays for a sick neighbor who then gets well. I have interviewed European and American doctors who work there as missionaries, and they admit that they have no scientific explanation for some amazing recoveries they have seen. David Aikman's book *Jesus in Beijing* reports a similar pattern of apparent miracles in China.

On the other hand, Christians in Nepal and China tell horrific stories of oppression, imprisonment, and torture. My Japanese friend introduced me to a Chinese pastor viewed as one of four patriarchs in the unregistered church, a giant of faith who spent twenty-three years in prison because he refused to halt his church activities. Pastor Yuan told me with great excitement of a miracle: during his long sentence in a prison near Mongolia, he worked daily outdoors wearing nothing but a light jacket in the harshest winter weather and never caught a common cold or influenza. I marveled at his story, but inwardly I could not help wondering why God answered that prayer and not the thousands of prayers from church members pleading for his release.

I asked my Japanese friend how to reconcile this strange combination of miraculous answers to prayer in the midst of intense persecution. If God can heal sick people or prevent illness, then why not protect suffering Christians? (As soon as I phrased the question, I had to smile, for that replicates the pattern of the book of Acts.) She thought for a moment and said, "I know this is a 'textbook' answer, but everything is in our Lord's hands. And he shows his glory in each occasion."

In all my prayers, whether I get the answers I want or not, I can count on this one fact: God can make use of whatever happens. Nothing is irredeemable. "Teach me, O God, so to use all the circumstances of my life today that they may bring forth in me the fruits of holiness rather than the fruits of sin," prayed the British author John Baillie:

> *Let me use disappointment as material for patience.*
> *Let me use success as material for thankfulness.*
> *Let me use trouble as material for perseverance.*
> *Let me use danger as material for courage.*
> *Let me use reproach as material for long suffering.*
> *Let me use praise as material for humility.*
> *Let me use pleasures as material for temperance.*
> *Let me use pain as material for endurance.*

By selfish nature I tend to pray for successes, happy outcomes, and relief from difficulties. And I must say, with gratitude, I have experienced my share of the good things life offers. But in the Beatitudes Jesus calls "blessed" those who experience the very opposite: poverty, mourning, hunger, persecution. How would my faith survive, and my prayers change, if life took a dramatic turn for the worse—if I came down with a degenerative disease or lost my home or landed in prison because of my beliefs? Could I fill in the blanks of John Baillie's prayers with details of my own newly lapsed state? Would I humbly allow the Spirit to accomplish God's purposes in me even through such unwelcome agents?

I have a book titled *Prayers of the Martyrs*, which reproduces actual prayers of martyrs from AD 107 (Ignatius of Antioch) to 1980 (Archbishop Oscar Romero). I find it shocking how few prayed for deliverance as in the background lions roared, gladiators sharpened their swords, or, in Romero's case, assassins fastened ammunition clips onto their automatic weapons. The martyrs prayed for families left behind, for steadfastness of faith, for strength to endure death without shame. Some thanked God for the privilege of suffering, surprised they would be counted worthy. Some forgave their persecutors. Very few asked for a miracle.

God's Smile

Theologian Ronald Goetz calls himself an "occasionist": God acts in response to prayer, he believes, but with baffling unpredictability. (Of course, most of us pray with baffling unpredictability, too.) Review the alternatives, though. God could act alone, ignoring us and our prayers. Or God could leave matters entirely in our hands with no direct involvement in human history. The first option contradicts the whole motive behind creating personal beings made in God's image; the second option is too ominous to contemplate.

We have, instead, a relationship with God based on constant negotiation. We inform God what we think should be done in the world, and in the process God reminds us of our own role in doing it. Rarely do we get everything we want, and I imagine the same holds true for God.

The trail of God at work rarely follows a straight line, which means our prayers may well produce different answers than we expect. For whatever reason—God's sense of irony, antagonistic spiritual powers, the vicissitudes of a fallen planet—prayers get answered in ways we could neither predict nor imagine.

Each December actors in Christmas pageants recite the jubilant responses of two cousins, the elderly infertile Elizabeth and the young virgin Mary, as they learn news of their surprise pregnancies. How must Mary have looked back on her great prayer, the Magnificat, as she saw Jesus crucified by the very rulers she had hoped he would vanquish? And Elizabeth's husband Zechariah, who had prophesied "salvation from our enemies and from the hand of all who hate us"—what did he think as he watched his son John grow into an insect-eating dissident who got beheaded by one of those enemies? Both families prayed fervently, and neither got the answer they expected.

Sometimes, though, an unanswered prayer opens the door to something far better. For fifteen years Monica prayed for her son Augustine as he indulged his senses and investigated exotic philosophies. When Augustine finally converted, these were the very experiences that gave depth and richness to his writings, allowing him to set the course of Christian thought for centuries. Once, Monica prayed all night that God would stop her son from going to wicked Rome, but he tricked her and sailed away. It was on that trip, in fact, that Augustine became a Christian. Reflecting later, he said that God denied his mother once in order to grant her what she had prayed for always.

Edith Schaeffer, the daughter of missionaries, tells of Dr. Hoste, the successor to Hudson Taylor as director of China Inland Mission, praying daily on a walk that lasted four hours. He counted that task his chief responsibility as leader of the mission and mentioned each missionary and child by name. Within a few years, however, Chairman Mao would evict all seven thousand missionaries from China, including all those for whom Hoste prayed. They relocated to places like the Philippines, Hong Kong, and Singapore, dismayed at what might happen to the fledgling church in China now bereft of outside help. In their absence, under a dictatorial regime that forbade Christian evangelism, the greatest numerical revival in history broke out. What happened in China, and is happening now, exceeds beyond all dreams the prayer requests of the missionaries of 1950.

"If you want to see God smile, tell him your plans," goes an old saying.

Human Agents

In answering prayers, God normally relies on human agents. On a visit to Holland I heard the story of strict Dutch Calvinist farmers who, during the devastating floods of the 1950s, climbed onto the roofs of their barns but refused to be rescued. "God's will be done," they said.

Someone made a joke about one such farmer who sat on his roof with floodwaters swirling around him. A neighbor in a rowboat offered him help, which he declined, insisting, "God will protect me." A helicopter buzzed overhead, its rescue party lowering a rope and ordering through a loudspeaker, "Grab the rope, and we'll pull you to safety." The farmer stubbornly shook his head no.

Soon the water engulfed the barn and swept the farmer away. In heaven he demanded an explanation from God. "I counted on you to protect me! Why didn't you answer my prayers?"

God replied, "I sent you a rowboat and then a helicopter. What more did you want?"

Those of us who struggle with unanswered prayer dare not overlook an important theological truth about how God acts in this world today. The church is the body of Christ, and as such it does God's work. As Ronald Rolheiser expresses it, "A theist believes in a God in heaven whereas a Christian believes in a God in heaven who is also physically present on this earth inside of human beings. . . . God is still present, as physical and as real today as God was in the historical Jesus. God still has skin, human skin, and physically walks on this earth just as Jesus did."

To pray "God, please help my neighbor cope with her financial problems," or "God, do something about the homeless downtown" is the approach of a theist, not a Christian. God has chosen to express love and grace in the world through those of us who embody Christ.

As a journalist I see this principle at work in inspiring ways. While writing this book I have made trips to several different countries. I visited a church in South Africa, 35,000 members strong, which runs outreach programs including a prison ministry, a hospital, and a rehabilitation farm for addicts. In the same city I visited a woman who recruits volunteers to come in daily and act as surrogate mothers to children afflicted with AIDS. Two months later I traveled to Nepal where I met with health workers from fifteen nations who serve under a mission specializing in leprosy work. Historically, most of the major advances in leprosy treatment have come from Christian missionaries—mainly because they were the only ones willing to treat the dreaded disease.

A few months later, in Wisconsin, I attended a conference on ministry to women in prostitution that attracted representatives from thirty different nations. They work to counter illegal sex trafficking and also to liberate women from prostitution, which in poor nations constitutes a modern form of slavery. From there I went to a Salvation Army conference where I heard stories from the world's third-largest standing "army"—this one mobilized to help the poor and downtrodden—then to Roanoke, Virginia, where I visited a sprawling complex that began as a rescue mission and, through the help of sixty churches, grew into a shelter, education center, and clinic.

As I interviewed the leaders of these ministries, I learned that many began with a crisis of faith, indeed a crisis of prayer. *God, why don't you do something about the homeless families in Roanoke . . . or the AIDS orphans in Johannesburg? Don't they break your heart?* Inevitably, there followed a prayer echoing the one prayed by Bob Pierce, founder of the global charity World Vision: "Lord, may my heart be broken by what breaks your heart." Those who responded became the answers to their own prayers.

Children view God as a celestial version of Santa Claus who sits on a cloud considering requests and funneling answers like presents down a chimney. A better model might be the president of a large corporation who must occasionally step in to manage a crisis but prefers to delegate tasks to trusted managers and employees. Or better yet, the metaphor the New Testament relies on: a human body, in which all parts of the body are organically joined and cooperate to carry out the will of the head.

An Apostle's Prayer

The apostle Paul had one overriding desire: that fellow Jews would embrace the Messiah he had encountered on the road to Damascus. "I have great sorrow and unceasing anguish in my heart," he said. "For I could wish that I myself were cursed and cut off from Christ for the sake of my brothers, those of my own race, the people of Israel." No doubt

Paul prayed to that end daily, yet seldom saw it answered. In city after city his fellow Jews rejected him and he turned to the Gentiles.

I see in Paul's response to that disappointment an ideal pattern of coping with an unanswered prayer. In the first place, he did not simply make a request and resign himself to God's decision. Paul the human agent put feet to his prayer, making a habit of going first to the synagogue when he entered a new town, often at great personal cost as his visits led to riots.

Furthermore, Paul persevered, even when it became increasingly clear that his prayer was not being answered. John Calvin said, "We must repeat the same supplications not twice or three times only, but as often as we have need, a hundred and a thousand times. . . . We must never be weary in waiting for God's help."

Apparently, however, Paul did grow weary. In his most elegant letter, he sets as his centerpiece (Romans 9–11) a passionate passage, a verbal wrestling match with God in which he struggles openly with this the great unanswered prayer of his life.

Paul acknowledges one important side benefit (the "surprise factor") of this most distressing development: the Jews' rejection of Jesus led to his acceptance by the Gentiles. It seems strange, he admits, that the Gentiles who did not pursue God's gift attained it whereas the Jews who did pursue it have not attained it—not yet, anyway.

Paul is trying to make sense of history, a very personal history. Sometimes his passion interrupts: "Brothers, my heart's desire and prayer to God for the Israelites is that they may be saved." He plows over the same ground, looking for something he may have missed. And he concludes that God hasn't rejected the Jews; to the contrary, they have the same opportunity as Gentiles. God has widened, not closed, the embrace of humanity.

The prose begins to soar as Paul steps back to consider the big picture. And then comes this burst of doxology in the midst of Paul's dissertation on an unanswered prayer:

Oh, the depth of the riches of the wisdom and knowledge of God!

> How unsearchable his judgments,
>> and his paths beyond tracing out!

> "Who has known the mind of the Lord?
>> Or who has been his counselor?"

> "Who has ever given to God,
>> that God should repay him?"

For from him and through him and to him are all things.

To him be the glory forever! Amen.

In a flash Paul has gained a glimpse of the view from the top of the mountain, not timberline, the view from Andromeda, not Rome.* In that glimpse, somehow the doleful events of history and theologians' mind-numbing theodicies, the unsolved mysteries and unanswered prayers all fade to grey against the Technicolor panorama of God's plan for the ages. God is the potter, we are the clay. God is the Father, we are the children.

Perhaps more accurately, God is the playwright, we are the actors. That prayer exists at all is a gift of grace, a generous invitation to participate in the future of the cosmos.

In the end, unanswered prayer brings me face-to-face with the mystery that silenced Paul: the profound difference between my perspective and God's.

> "For my thoughts are not your thoughts,
>> neither are your ways my ways,"
>> declares the Lord.

---

* William Sloane Coffin says of this passage about God's unsearchable judgments, "Christianity is less a set of beliefs than a way of life, and a way of life that actually warns against absolute intellectual certainty."

"As the heavens are higher than the earth,
   so are my ways higher than your ways
   and my thoughts than your thoughts."

A Senior Citizen's Prayer

As I was writing this chapter, my wife recommended that I interview some senior citizens about prayer. "Most of them pray, and they've been at it a long time," she said. "Surely they'll have some wisdom for you."

She was right. I accompanied her to the retirement center where she assists as a chaplain, and that morning I heard one miracle story after another. One of the seniors had felt a sudden urge to leave a card game and go home. As she walked in the door she saw that a candle had burned to the nub, igniting a bouquet of plastic roses—a fire she was able to smother with a pillow just in time. Another told of remarkable survival stories from World War II. Another told of her husband choking on a homemade cinnamon roll, just as two paramedics walked past who saved his life by performing the Heimlich maneuver.

I heard, too, of prayers for world peace and against injustice. Those prayers saw seniors through the scary times of a world war and then a cold war that threatened the very survival of the species. One African-American senior reminisced about praying while growing up as a second-class citizen in the South. Who could imagine then the changes she would live through?

Although I probed for accounts of unanswered prayers, most of the seniors preferred to talk about answered prayers. All of them could tell of family tragedies and health breakdowns, but somehow these events did not shake their faith in prayer.

After our meeting, however, I wandered through a portion of the facility that cares for seniors who need more assistance. They lay in beds or sat in wheelchairs. One man was so slouched over that his chin rested on the wheelchair tray. Some wore orthopedic boots, some hummed nervously, some drooled, some snored. One woman with a vacant stare waved a banana in her hand. Another repeated the same phrase over and over. I tried talking to these seniors, too, but the lights in their minds had gone out. Any secrets they had learned about prayer lay hidden beyond retrieval.

I drove away from the facility more convinced than ever that the only final solution to unanswered prayer is Paul's explanation to the Corinthians: "For now we see through a glass, darkly; but then face to face: now I know in part; but then shall I know even as also I am known." No human being, no matter how wise or how spiritual, can interpret the ways of God, explain why one miracle and not another, why an apparent intervention here and not there. Along with the apostle Paul, we can only wait, and trust.

~ What to Pray For

We do not want to be beginners [at prayer].

But let us be convinced of the fact that we will never be anything
but beginners, all our life!

—THOMAS MERTON

UNANSWERED PRAYERS AND UNANSWERED questions about God and physical healing can leave us feeling confused and mute about the requests we present. What exactly should we pray for?

From interviews with suffering people and ordinary pray-ers, from the experience of caregivers, chaplains, and helpers, I have gathered the following guidelines on prayer. They offer a template of how to pray, not only for a person who suffers but for all of us who cry out to God at a time of need. These prayers we can count on, and pray with confidence.

Heart Desire

I have learned to tell God exactly what I want regardless of how impossible it may sound. I pray for peace in the Middle East, for justice in Africa, for religious freedom in China and other countries, for an end to homelessness and racism in the U.S., because I earnestly desire those things—and moreover, I believe God does too.

A friend of mine in Chicago tried to recruit some colleagues in urban ministry to join him in a season of prayer for an end to poverty in that city. Almost everyone he asked balked. "Why pray for something so idealistic and impossible?" they objected. My friend had a different view. What is the point of prayer if not to express our heart's desire, especially when it matches what we know to be God's will on earth? Who knows what will happen when we pray what we know God desires? Remember the many prayers of Christians behind the Iron Curtain and in an apartheid South Africa, prayers that also seemed impossible and idealistic.

God invites us to ask plainly for what we need. We will not be scolded any more than a child who climbs into her parent's lap and presents a Christmas wish list. Dr. Vernon Grounds says that when he hears of someone in need of healing, he prays like this: "God, I know you have your own purposes and undoubtedly have a plan for this person, but I'll tell you straight out what I would like to see happen."

If diagnosed with a serious illness, I would ask directly for physical healing. We are commanded to pray for healing, Jesus decisively demonstrated God's desire for human health and wholeness, and dozens of studies have borne out the effectiveness of prayer in the healing process. Faith works. It aligns body, mind, and spirit, and galvanizes the healing processes built into our bodies.

Sometimes Jesus asked a person, "Do you want to be healed?" That was no idle question: as doctors testify, some patients can hardly imagine an identity apart from their unwell condition. In prayers for healing, as in all prayers of request, we should honestly present the problem and tell God our heart's desire.

Lament

"Lord, the one you love is sick," Mary and Martha informed Jesus about their brother Lazarus in a form of prayer. Preachers like to accent the personality differences between the scurrying, type A Martha and her contemplative sister Mary. What strikes me in the story is their twin response to Jesus when he shows up, apparently too late to help Lazarus. "Lord, if you had been here, my brother would not have died," Martha says after rushing out to meet Jesus. A while later, at a slower pace Mary arrives and says: "Lord, if you had been here, my brother would not have died." Suffering and grief cut across personality differences and reduce us all to lamenters. Sometimes we have nothing to offer in our prayers but complaint.

Jesus' response follows, not a rebuke but a spasm of compassion ("he was deeply moved in spirit and troubled") punctuated by the shortest verse in the Bible: "Jesus wept."

A man who serves as the grief pastor of a large church in Colorado reminds me of the value of tears. John spends much of his time visiting the sick and dying, and most weeks he conducts at least one funeral. In addition, he has two children of his own with life-threatening genetic disorders. "Evangelicals tend to want to get to the happy ending," John says. "Sometimes there is no happy ending, and we're simply suspended in grief. When I'm with suffering people, I feel like a deep-sea diver accompanying them into the depths. Come up too fast, and you'll dangerously decompress. We need to stay with the grief for a while, feel it, let it out. Maybe we can see things through tears that we can't see dry-eyed."

Not only does God tolerate complaint in our prayers, the Scriptures fill in the words for us. Eugene Peterson calculates that two-thirds of the psalms qualify as laments. The Bible does not rush to a happy ending.

A dead-end marriage that seems to offer no way out. A surly teenager who saps the family finances and shows resentment, not appreciation. A spouse who has no interest in sex. Global terrorism. A national election that goes the wrong way. A bitter and divided church. A parent with dementia. Each of these circumstances rightly calls for prayers of lament.

Robertson McQuilkin, as patient a man as I know, confessed the temptation to scream at, even slap, his Alzheimer's-afflicted wife when irritation reached a certain level. Prayer offers a better alternative, just as the psalms' fierce prayers against enemies offer a better alternative than personal revenge. We need feel no guilt over such prayers of frustration, for God welcomes them.

Confession

Sin can disrupt the relationship between ourselves and God in a way that jars the alignment of body, soul, and spirit. Confession restores the channel of communication with God while at the same time flushing away anxiety, guilt, fear, and other obstacles to health.

I have mentioned the inner conversation that we all conduct at a level inaudible to those around us. When I struggle with guilt, I find that inner conversation revolving around myself: attempts to rationalize or explain away my behavior, resentment against others who caused it, feelings of self-pity and remorse. Only confession can clear away that self-absorption and open my spirit to God's soft voice.

Ed Dobson, the well-known pastor of Calvary Church in Grand Rapids, Michigan, grappled with confession after contracting the terminal disease ALS. "When I was diagnosed, I thought, *If I'm going to die, I want to die with a clear conscience and whole relationships.* I knew there were people I had offended, people I needed to ask for forgiveness. So I made a list and began calling."

Dobson had his roots in the fundamentalist movement and in right-wing Moral Majority politics but later moved in a different direction, especially in his outreach to the local homosexual community. When he learned of his illness he called colleagues from the past—Jerry Falwell, Bob Jones, James Dobson (no relation)—and asked for forgiveness if he had offended them. After that, he prayed with a clear conscience and sensed a new freedom in his prayers.

Clearing obstructions in a relationship with God allows us to take a giant step toward wholeness and health. And we can have confidence that a prayer of confession God will always answer, with guaranteed forgiveness. Writes the apostle John, "But if anybody does sin, we have one who speaks to the Father in our defense—Jesus Christ, the Righteous One."

Jaime Cardinal Sin, the Catholic archbishop of Manila who played a key role in the People Power revolution there, liked to tell the story of a woman who attended his weekly audience to inform him she had a message from God. He brushed her off several times, but she kept coming back. Finally he said, "We Catholics have strict rules governing visions and messages from God. I need to test your authenticity. I want you to go back and ask God about a particular sin I recently confessed in private. If you ask God and he tells you the answer, I'll know your vision is genuine."

The next week she returned and he quizzed her, a bit nervously, "Well, did you ask God about my sin?"

"I did."

"And did God answer?"

"Yes."

"What did he say?"

"God said that he couldn't remember."

Peace

Roy Lawrence, a vicar and adviser on prayer to a British bishop, says that we make a mistake to think that effective prayer must involve great effort. "We think of it as hard work, as striving. . . . That is the way I myself used to think. In fact, often after praying for somebody's healing, I would find the imprints of my own nails on my palms because I had been clenching my fists so tightly as I agonized in prayer."

Lawrence became convinced that prayer has more to do with resting than with striving. "Come to me, all you who are weary and burdened, and I will give you rest," Jesus said—or, as another translation has it, "and I will refresh you." For guidance on prayer, Lawrence now looks to the passage in John 15 in which Jesus holds up the image of a vine and branches. The branch bears fruit not by striving or agonizing, simply by "abiding" or resting.

I wrote earlier about changing the direction of prayer. Rather than begin with my own requests and demands, I can begin with God, first getting to know who God is and then positioning myself in the stream of God's own love and power. When praying for a person who is sick or troubled, I try to begin not by presenting a list of requests, as urgent as they may be, but rather by meditating on how God must already feel about the person I am praying for.

I know how God feels because of Jesus: I see the tears of compassion he wept for Mary and Martha; I see the physical healing Jesus provided every time he was asked; I see the transformations he worked in prostitutes and tax collectors and social outcasts. I gain peace when I realize that I do not have to talk God into caring. God cares more than I can imagine, and has ultimate control over all that happens.

"Peace I leave with you; my peace I give you," Jesus told his disciples. Any doctor will agree that the absence of peace, in the form of stress, fear, tension, or worry, endangers physical health as much as a disease microbe. The persecuted church also needs peace. Parents of newborns need peace. College students need peace. Caregivers and relief workers in the world's hot spots need peace. As a farewell gift, the Prince of Peace presented to us the one thing we most need on a turbulent planet.

How exactly should you pray in a given circumstance? Will your prayers lead to divine healing, or should you rather come to terms with a chronic, even terminal condition? Will you get released from prison or should you look for ways to redeem the time? Should you pursue intensive premarital counseling or simply break off the engagement? Again, Paul's soothing promise about the Spirit relieves that pressure, making possible peace in the midst of confusion:

> In the same way, the Spirit helps us in our weakness. We do not know what we ought to pray for, but the Spirit himself intercedes for us with groans that words cannot express. And he who searches our hearts knows the mind of the Spirit, because the Spirit intercedes for the saints in accordance with God's will.

God's Presence

In the same Last Supper conversation in which Jesus bequeathed his peace, he also promised a far greater gift: the presence of God, who would live not in some faraway heaven but inside us, in our very souls.

He promised us the Holy Spirit, and the title he chose, the Counselor (or Comforter), itself indicates one of the Spirit's main roles. The *sense* of God's presence may come and go. Yet the believer can have confidence that God is already present, living inside, and need not be summoned from afar.

I have seen evidence of God's presence in the most unexpected places. During our trip to Nepal, a physical therapist gave my wife and me a tour of the Green Pastures Hospital, which specializes in leprosy rehabilitation. As we walked along an outdoor corridor, I noticed in a courtyard one of the ugliest human beings I have ever seen. Her hands were bandaged in gauze, she had deformed stumps where most people have feet, and her face showed the worst ravages of that cruel disease. Her nose had shrunken away so that, looking at her, I could see into her sinus cavity. Her eyes, mottled and covered with callus, let in no light; she was totally blind. Scars covered patches of skin on her arms.

We toured a unit of the hospital and returned along the same corridor. In the meantime this creature had crawled across the courtyard to the very edge of the walkway, pulling herself along the ground by planting her elbows and dragging her body like a wounded animal. I'm ashamed to say my first thought was, *She's a beggar. She wants money.* My wife, who has worked among the down-and-out, had a much more holy reaction. Without hesitation she bent down to the woman and put her arm around her. The old woman rested her head against Janet's shoulder and began singing a song in Nepali, a tune that we all instantly recognized: "Jesus loves me, this I know, for the Bible tells me so."

"Danmaya is one of our most devoted church members," the physical therapist later told us. "Most of our patients are Hindus, but we have a little Christian chapel here, and Danmaya comes every time the door opens. She's a prayer warrior. She loves to greet and welcome every visitor who comes to Green Pastures, and no doubt she heard us talking as we walked along the corridor."

A few months later we heard that Danmaya had died. Close to my desk I keep a photo that I snapped just as she was singing to Janet.

Whenever I feel polluted by the beauty-obsessed celebrity culture I live in—a culture in which people pay exorbitant sums to shorten their noses or plump up their breasts to achieve some impossible ideal of beauty while nine thousand people die each day from AIDS for lack of treatment and hospitals like Green Pastures scrape by on charity crumbs—I pull out that photo. I see two beautiful women: my wife, smiling sweetly, wearing a brightly colored Nepali outfit she had bought the day before, holding in her arms an old crone who would flunk any beauty test ever devised except the one that matters most. Out of that deformed, hollow shell of a body, the light of God's presence shines out. The Holy Spirit found a home.

Compassion

During hard times my vision narrows so that I think only of myself and my problems. Then, more than ever, I need to widen that vision, to expand the circle of God's love. I need to review Paul's words about God who comforts us "so that we can comfort those in any trouble with the comfort we ourselves have received from God." I need to remember that the weakness and discomfort I feel temporarily, some people must cope with every day.

I used to spend a lot of energy asking God questions. Why must poverty persist in a rich country like the U.S.A.? Why does one continent, Africa, absorb like a sponge so many of the world's disasters? When will "peace on earth" ever arrive? Ultimately, I came to see these questions as God's interrogations of us. Jesus made clear God's will for the planet—what part am I playing to help fulfill that will?

When I pray for the healing of AIDS in Africa, I pray for the campaigns by World Vision and World Concern and Tear Fund to raise awareness, for the rock star Bono and his prophetic challenge to the church, for the boards of the pharmaceutical companies as they make sacrificial decisions to donate drugs, for government leaders as they debate funding, for doctors and relief workers and educators on the ground in Africa who minister directly to patients and scout out homes for orphans. In this small way, through my prayers, I contribute.

When I pray for my friends with debilitating diseases such as Alzheimer's and ALS, I try to remember to pray also for the caregivers who bear many of the same stresses, and sometimes bear abuse as well. I pray for their strength and courage and their long-term endurance. Most caregivers tell of a burst of support from relatives, friends, and church members at the onset of the condition. Over time, such support tends to fade away: because of a weak theology of suffering, many churches tend to view unhealed people as an embarrassment, a token of failure.

I also pray for practical resources: provision for the physical needs of life, for meals and volunteer helpers and medical insurance and financial help. Of course, as I pray those prayers I also have to listen for God's message to me. Should I actively join the stream of God's love and comfort? Should I become one of those helpers? (Of the accounts of individuals being healed in the Gospels, all but seven were brought to Jesus by someone else.) To pray is a dangerous act.

For some people, illness itself may prevent much direct activity. But at least we can pray. After three devastating strokes the author Corrie ten Boom, formerly a globetrotting "tramp for the Lord," found herself confined to bed in a single room overlooking a garden. She had her helpers mount photos of friends and missionaries on every wall. Even when her limbs no longer functioned, her eyes moved from one photo to another and others in the room knew what that meant: Corrie was praying.

Gratitude

Life is a gift. I heard a stirring speech from a young man, David Rothenberg, who has undergone more than sixty major surgeries and faces the prospect of scores more. As a six-year-old he suffered third-degree burns over 90 percent of his body when his father gave him a sleeping pill, poured kerosene over him, and set him afire. What gives you the courage to keep going? he was asked. David replied, "I am alive! I am alive! I am alive! I didn't miss out on living and that is good enough for me."

Medical research is discovering that gratitude is the one emotional trait most likely to benefit physical health and recovery. Grateful people tend to be happier and more satisfied with their lives, and may actually live longer. "A grateful heart might be a healthy heart," one researcher concluded after studying the effect of gratitude on relieving stress and hypertension.

I have a vivid memory of two back-to-back nights in Chicago. One evening I met with a good friend who informed me she was leaving her husband, also a close friend. "He doesn't meet my needs," she said. "I know he tries to be a good husband and good father, but I've found someone better. I'm leaving him." After listening to her, I talked about the difficulties all marriages face and reminded her of many of her husband's good qualities and all that she would be losing. She agreed with everything I said but had already made up her mind. I left that meal with a heavy heart, knowing my wife and I had lost one of our best couple friendships.

The very next night I attended a celebration organized by a young widow whose husband had died of brain cancer. On the night that would have been Chuck's thirty-second birthday, she was holding a party in his memory. I knew the agony they had been through during his surgery and prolonged treatment. Lynne now faced the double burden of paying off medical bills and supporting two children as a single mother. Still reeling from the news of my friend's impending divorce, I went to Lynne's house with a sense of foreboding.

I heard not a word of complaint or regret that night. Lynne passed around photos and had each of us call up memories of her husband. We laughed, and cried, and Lynne pulled out a guitar and sang some of his favorite songs. She talked about the good times they had shared together, his corny jokes, the cartoons he drew, the intimacy of walking together through the progression of his illness. "I will always miss him," she said, "but I'll always be grateful for the exciting few years we shared together. Chuck was a gift to me."

On consecutive nights I saw a stark difference in two approaches to life. One resents loss and wants more. One celebrates life as a gift, something to remember with gratitude. I ask God for that spirit regardless of my circumstances.

Faith

The Bible puts forward two different kinds of faith. The one kind—bold, childlike faith—impressed Jesus, and several times such faith from the most unlikely sources "astonished" him. Another kind, I term *fidelity*, a hang-on-by-the-fingernails faith against all odds, no matter the cost. Abraham, Joseph, Job, and others of God's favorites in the Old Testament demonstrated this faith, and the tribute in Hebrews 11 honors them.

Scientific studies have amply proved the value of positive, hopeful faith on overall health. A belief in healing, in transcendent power, has a salutary effect on the body's actual cells. Millions can testify to that effect.

For others, however, there comes a time when it seems clear that no amount of faith will gain the desired healing. "I have lived with Crohn's disease for twenty-three years," writes Stephen Schmidt. "I know the disappointment, the rage, the ongoing reality that I will not get better. Period."

> So I come to the question of prayer with a very personal bias. I can pray my heart out and shout my defiance into eternity, but I will not be healed of Crohn's disease, at least not now, until some new medical insight or drug is found. I have stopped asking God for a miracle. That has not happened for me in twenty-three years, and for whatever length of time I still have to be and live, it is not helpful, reasonable, or faithful to ask of God that which is not possible. That would be magic. I am too old for magic, too experienced for sentimentality, and too angry and frustrated to waste time on a specific kind of prayer which in my life would be a prayerful placebo, practicing the piety of prayerful impossibility.

Schmidt goes on to say that he has accepted suffering as part of being human. He had to be healed of the need to be healed. Now he prays for strength to endure, for meaning in his suffering, for faith to believe in a good and loving God even when he has to go in once again for a painful surgical procedure. Each day he must live out fidelity faith.

As I have admitted, I need more of the childlike faith that impressed Jesus. By temperament I accept too readily what life throws me and start to make adjustments. Instead, I should ask God for the vision to see what can be changed.

For all its benefits, though, childlike faith has one major flaw: it stakes everything on the future, on a desired change. For some, that change never comes. If you wait until you are well or employed or married or whatever new state you are asking for, you may never get there. I have learned that I have no time in which to live out Christ's life other than *now*. This very moment is all I can count on.

In one of his letters Paul described himself as afflicted but not crushed, perplexed but not driven to despair, persecuted but not forsaken, struck down but not destroyed. He learned a different level of faith, one that does not remove difficulty but nevertheless withstands, a fidelity in which weakness transforms into strength and prayers for healing melt into prayers of acceptance.

Grace

By definition no one deserves grace and yet it descends, dropping "as the gentle rain from heaven," to borrow Shakespeare's comment about mercy. In response, human spirits ascend beyond heights they could ever achieve on their own.

Grace allowed Nelson Mandela to emerge from twenty-seven years of prison with a spirit of magnanimity and reconciliation, rather than the resentment and revenge to which he was entitled.

Grace allowed George Chen, arrested for his "barefoot evangelist" activities in China, to find a most unlikely prayer closet while serving an eighteen-year sentence at hard labor. Guards forced him to work in the prison cesspool, where he spent his days knee-deep in human waste, turning it with a shovel to make compost. "They thought I'd be miserable, but actually I was happy," said Chen. "It smelled so bad that no one could come near me, so I could pray and sing aloud all day."

Grace allows the mother of a severely disabled child to live without the self-pity such a state might normally produce. A woman in Michigan told me of her son, born with spina bifida and hydrocephalus, who requires constant care. The financial burden alone caused her to abandon most of her dreams. Yet, she told me, "Though my son has never spoken a word, no master of theology could teach more about unconditional love."

By mentioning this woman I do not wish to compound the guilt of a mother who might wake up every day resenting the demands of her child and blaming God for the curse of disability. Grace descends as the gentle rain from heaven. It does not divide, does not rank. It floats like a cloud high in the sky, and the thirsty pray for it as desert nomads pray for rain.

One man daily grows embittered by his paralysis; another prays for the grace to cope. One abused child harbors hatred and resentment; another rejoices that "I am alive!" One estranged family lets the walls remain in place; another begins the laborious task of dismantling them. Prayer for grace offers the chance for a deep healing, or at least a way to cope with what cannot be fixed.

Lee Van Ham, a Presbyterian pastor, kept a prayer journal during a battle with testicular cancer. At first he wrote many pages, both listening and talking to God during the initial shock of illness. After surgery, the communication simply stopped. He leaned on the prayers of others but found no ability to pray himself. He began to lose heart, overwhelmed with grief at the prospect of life that would likely be cut short before his children grew up and before grandchildren arrived.

"How do I live these days of low energy in which I'm more aware of having to let go of things than doing them?" he prayed, asking the same question over and over. One day an answer came: "With love. With great love."

> I began to practice doing the simple things with love. I loaded and unloaded the dishwasher with thoughts of love. It was very different from thoughts such as "If I didn't have to do dishes, I could do more important things." Or, "It seems I'm doing more than my share of this mundane stuff." I practiced waiting in love while the computer started up instead of fidgeting and scolding the machine's sloth. On days when I could drive, yellow lights at the intersections became reminders to brake, to stop and to refocus my life in love, not accelerate and hurry. . . .
>
> I realized how dark the theater had been for several weeks. Now it was apparent that in that darkness and in the vast emptiness behind the stage of my soul, God had been forming divine and eternal thoughts to present to me: "With love, Lee. Live these days with great love." It chanted inside of me many times throughout the day . . . and still does.

Grace had descended on a parsonage in Illinois. It followed Lee to California, where he serves a new parish, with love. Through illness, he learned an attitude that can last a lifetime.

Preparations

Flannery O'Connor, a brilliant writer struck down before the age of forty after a battle with lupus, lamented, "I have never been anywhere but sick. In a sense sickness is a place, more instructive than a long trip to Europe, and it's always a place where there's no company, where nobody can follow." She added these words, amazing in light of the suffering she endured: "Sickness before death is a very appropriate thing and I think those who don't have it miss one of God's mercies."

Not everyone will reach the exalted plateau of acceptance shown in those words. We go through stages and manifest the works of God in distinct and unique ways. Sometimes we never attain the faith for which we strive. And that is why we pray. As a prayer in the Roman Missal states it, "May what comes to us in our time be for our healing in the everlasting years. Amen."

The apostle Paul described a personal dilemma. As he sat in a Roman prison, reflecting on all the hardships he had endured, death loomed as a welcome relief. At least he would be with Christ, which is far better. At least his "eternal glory" would outweigh all the troubles. At least he would get a new body, healed of stripes and bruises. He had one prayer, that "Christ will be exalted in my body, whether by life or by death." Paul had found a way to fulfill Jesus' command, "do not worry about your life." He had come to terms with mortality and had no obsession with physical health. He realized that the time we spend on earth, with all its joys and griefs, triumphs and failures, is mere preparation. Paul was ready to die.

I have mentioned that my wife worked for a time as a hospice chaplain. A hospice has a 100 percent mortality rate; just to be admitted, a patient must have a doctor's diagnosis of advanced terminal disease. On average, most patients in this hospice lived less than two weeks. Working in a hospice affects one's view of life and health, Janet found, and especially it affects a way of praying. Imminent death offers a chance for old wounds to be healed, grudges forgiven, legacies passed on. Sometimes that happens, sometimes it doesn't.

Janet found that the obstacles to a good death were the very same obstacles to physical health: anxiety, tension, worry, guilt, fear. She sought to help patients express these emotions and come to terms with them. And for patients of faith, she saw the actual, practical help of belief in an afterlife, especially its promise of reunion with the loved ones who preceded and those who will follow.

For everyone death involves a process of letting go. Attachments, relatives, friendships, possessions, identity—everything that defines life for us, we let go in death. For a person in hospice, the deadline most of us try to ignore forces itself into view.

For the Christian, death also involves an anticipation of new beginning. We let go bodies that have served us, not perfectly but well enough, in exchange for new bodies. We let go a known life, touched with grace and pleasure but also evil and pain, in exchange for the promise of a life perfected. We let go the muddle of doctrine and wavering faith in exchange for sure knowledge at last. And during the rest of life we prepare for that exchange.

～ Resources

Our Deepest Longing

Epigraph: Albert Einstein, cited in *Leadership Journal* (Winter 1983), 43.

pg. 11: *"red corner"*: David Remnick, *Lenin's Tomb* (New York: Random House, 1993), 81.

pg. 11: *Pravda:* Quoted in Paul Johnson, *Modern Times* (New York: Harper & Row, 1983), 454.

pg. 12: *Merton:* Thomas Merton, quoted in Mark E. Thibodeaux, S.J., *Armchair Mystic* (Cincinnati: St. Anthony Messenger, 2001), ix.

pg. 12: *Gallup:* George H. Gallup, Jr., *Religion in America 1996* (Princeton, N.J.: The Princeton Religion Research Center, 1996), 4, 12, 19.

pg. 12: *Edwards:* Jonathan Edwards, quoted in Austin Phelps, *The Still Hour* (Carlisle, Penna.: Banner of Truth Trust, 1979), 11.

pg. 13: *Küng:* Hans Küng, cited in Ben Patterson, *Deepening Your Conversation with God*, Chapter 2, n.p., *www. ctlibrary. com/lebooks*.

pg. 14: *Buttrick:* George Buttrick, *Prayer* (New York: Abingdon, 1942), 26.

pg. 15: *Lloyd-Jones:* Martyn Lloyd-Jones, *Why Does God Allow War* (Wheaton, Ill.: Crossway, 2003), 15.

pg. 15: *May:* Gerald May, *Addiction & Grace* (San Francisco: HarperSanFrancisco, 1988), 1.

View from Above

Epigraph: George Marshall, source unknown.

pg. 19: *"One of the psalms . . . thunder":* Psalm 29:3.

pg. 19: *"Let me know":* Psalm 39:4.

pg. 20: *"When I consider":* Psalm 8:3 – 4.

pg. 20: *"O Lord":* Psalm 8:1.

pg. 21: *"Where were you":* Job 38:4.

pg. 21: *"Who is this":* Job 38:2.

pg. 22: *"[God] is not far":* Acts 17:27.

pg. 22: *Wilder:* Thornton Wilder, "Our Town," from *Three Plays* (New York: Harper & Brothers, 1957), Act 1, 45.

pg. 23: *"Let justice roll":* Amos 5:24.

pg. 23: *"Poor, bare":* Shakespeare, *King Lear*, 3.4, line 106.

pg. 24: *Schmemann:* Alexander Schmemann, cited in Alan Jones, *Soul Making* (San Francisco: Harper & Row, 1985), 53.

pg. 24: *"Be still":* Psalm 46:10.

pg. 24: (footnote) *Merton:* Thomas Merton, quoted in Ronald Rolheiser, *The Shattered Lantern* (New York: Crossroad, 2001), 40.

pg. 25: *Hampl:* Hampl, *Virgin*, op. cit., 217.

pg. 25: *"Know that":* Psalm 46:10.

pg. 25: (footnote) *"Almighty God":* cited in Jonathan Aitken, *Prayers for People Under Pressure* (London: Continuum, 2005), 176.

pg. 26: *"You would have":* John 19:11.

pg. 26: *Tugwell:* Simon Tugwell, *Prayer: Living with God* (Springfield, Ill.: Templegate Publishers, 1975), 35.

pg. 26: *Milton:* John Milton, *Paradise Lost*, Book VIII, line 103.

Why Pray?

Epigraph: R.S. Thomas, "Folk Tale," in *Experimenting with an Amen* (London: Macmillan, 1986), 53.

pg. 31: *Tolstoy:* Leo Tolstoy, *War and Peace* (Baltimore: Penguin, 1957), Vol. 1, 588.

pg. 32: *"One professor":* Quoted in Nancey Murphy, "Of Miracles," *Bulletin of the Center for Theology and the Natural Sciences*, vol. 10, no. 2 (Spring 1990), 16.

pg. 36: *"Now my heart":* John 12:27.

pg. 36: *"Abba":* Mark 14:36.

pg. 36: *"Eloi"*: Mark 15:34.

pg. 36: *"Offered up prayers"*: Hebrews 5:7.

pg. 36: *"Take this cup"*: Mark 14:36.

pg. 36: *"The people"*: John 11:42.

pg. 36: *"Father, forgive"*: Luke 23:34.

pg. 37: *"I have food"*: John 4:32.

pg. 37: *"Counselor"*: John 14:16.

pg. 38: *"skeptical Greeks"*: Joachim Jeremias, *The Prayers of Jesus*, op. cit., 66.

pg. 38: *"Anyone"*: John 14:9.

pg. 38: *" Your will"*: Matthew 6:10.

pg. 38: *"O unbelieving"*: Mark 9:19.

pg. 38: *"Do not put"*: Matthew 4:7.

pg. 39: *"My God, my God"*: Matthew 27:46.

pg. 39: (footnote) *Rousseau:* Jean-Jacques Rousseau, quoted in Harry Emerson Fosdick, *The Meaning of Prayer* (New York: Association Press, 1917), 62.

pg. 39: *"Ask"*: John 16:24.

pg. 39: *"That all of them"*: John 17:21.

pg. 40: *"Jesus went out"*: Luke 6:12.

pg. 40: *"Judas Iscariot"*: Luke 6:16.

pg. 40: *"Satan"*: Matthew 16:23.

pg. 40: *"How long"*: Matthew 17:17.

pg. 40: *Anderson:* Ray S. Anderson, *The Gospel According to Judas* (Colorado Springs: Helmers & Howard, 1991), 51 – 53.

pg. 40: *"Follow in his steps"*: 1 Peter 2:21.

pg. 41: *"Simon, Simon"*: Luke 22:31.

pg. 41: *"Then Satan"*: Luke 22:3.

pg. 42: *"Friend, do"*: Matthew 26:50.

pg. 42: *"Quench not"*: 1 Thessalonians 5:19 KJV.

pg. 42: *"Grieve not"*: Ephesians 4:30 KJV.

pg. 42: *Donne:* John Donne, "Divine Meditation 14" from *The Complete English Poems* (New York: Penguin, 1987), 314.

pg. 43: *"Do you think"*: Matthew 26:53.

pg. 43: *"Abba, Father . . . what you will"*: Mark 14:36.

pg. 44: *"You would have"*: John 19:11.

pg. 44: *Robinson:* Haddon Robinson, in *Focal Point* magazine, quoted by Paul Robbins in "The Back Page," *Leadership*, vol. 8 (1987), n.p.

pg. 45: *"O Jerusalem"*: Matthew 23:37.

pg. 46: *"For the joy"*: Hebrews 12:2.

pg. 46: *"Therefore he is able"*: Hebrews 7:24-25.

pg. 46: (footnote) *"And then the lawless"*: 2 Thessalonians 2:8.

Ask, Seek, Knock

Epigraph: *Milton:* John Milton, *Paradise Lost*, book XI, lines 307 – 10.

pg. 49: (footnote) *Bailey:* Kenneth Bailey, *Poet & Peasant* and *Through Peasant Eyes* (Grand Rapids, Mich.: Eerdmans, 1983), *Poet & Peasant*, 122.

pg. 50: *"Who watches over you"*: Psalm 121:3.

pg. 51: *"To show them"*: Luke 18:1.

pg. 51: *Bailey:* Kenneth Bailey, *Poet & Peasant* and *Through Peasant Eyes*. Page 134 of *Through Peasant Eyes* quoting H. B. Tristram, *Eastern Customs in Bible Lands* (London: Hodder and Stoughton, 1894), 228ff.

pg. 52: *"Even though I don't fear"*: Luke 18:4-5.

pg. 53: *"Where is this 'coming' "*: 2 Peter 3:4.

pg. 53: *Thielicke:* Helmut Thielicke, *Christ and the Meaning of Life* (Grand Rapids, Mich.: Baker Book House, 1975), 85.

pg. 54: *"Gates of hell"*: Matthew 16:18 KJV.

pg. 55: *Sittser:* Jerry Sittser, *When God Doesn't Answer Your Prayer* (Grand Rapids, Mich.: Zondervan, 2003), 115.

pg. 55: *"Lord, if you had"*: John 11:21.

pg. 55: *"Send her away"*: Matthew 15:23.

pg. 56: *Kierkegaard:* Søren Kierkegaard, quoted in Zaleski, *Prayer*, op. cit., 99.

pg. 57: *Cicero:* Cicero, quoted in A. L. Lilley, *Prayer and Christian Theology* (London: Billing & Sons Ltd., 1924), 4.

pg. 57: *MacDonald:* George MacDonald, *Creation in Christ* (Wheaton, Ill.: Harold Shaw, 1976), 315.

pg. 58: *Nouwen:* *"Why should I"*: Henri Nouwen, *Primacy of the Heart* (Madison, Wis.: St. Benedict Center, 1988), 9.

pg. 58: *Nouwen:* *"We must pray"*: Henri Nouwen, *The Road to Daybreak* (New York: Doubleday, 1988), 117.

pg. 58: *Nouwen:* *"Sitting in the presence"*: Henri Nouwen, *Primacy*, op. cit., 9.

pg. 58: *Weil:* Simone Weil, *The Notebooks of Simone Weil*, vol. 2 (New York: Putnam, 1956), 574.

pg. 59: *Augustine:* St. Augustine, quoted in Friedrich Heiler, *Prayer*, op. cit., 200.

pg. 59: *"If you then":* Luke 11:13; Matthew 7:11 (emphasis mine).

pg. 60: *"For we are":* Ephesians 2:10.

Yearning for Fluency

Epigraph: *Nouwen:* Henri Nouwen, *Reaching Out* (New York: Doubleday, 1975), 126.

pg. 63: *Buechner:* Frederick Buechner, *Now & Then* (San Francisco: Harper & Row, 1983), 32.

pg. 65: *"Teach us to pray":* Luke 11:1.

pg. 65: *Teresa:* Mother Teresa, *Everything Starts*, op. cit., 39, 40.

pg. 65: *Weatherhead:* Leslie Weatherhead, *A Private House of Prayer* (Nashville: Abingdon, 1958), 28.

pg. 66: *Nouwen:* Henri Nouwen, *The Genesee Diary* (Garden City, N.Y.: Image Books/Doubleday, 1981), 140.

pg. 67: *Postema:* Don Postema, *Space for God* (Grand Rapids, Mich.: Bible Way/CRC Publications, 1983), 17.

pg. 67: *Morford:* Judy Morford, quoted in Terry Muck, *Liberating the Leader's Prayer Life* (Carol Stream, Ill.: Christianity Today/Word Books, 1985), 67.

pg. 69: *Yankelovich:* Daniel Yankelovich, cited in Joseph M. Champlin, *Behind Closed Doors: A Handbook on How to Pray* (New York: Paulist Press, 1984), 63 – 4.

pg. 69: *"Full armor":* Ephesians 6:11.

pg. 71: *Virgil:* Cited in Simon Tugwell, *Prayer*, op. cit., 5.

pg. 71: *"Blessed are the pure":* Matthew 5:8.

pg. 72: *"Renewing":* see Romans 12:2.

pg. 73: *Nouwen:* Henri Nouwen, quoted in Terry Muck, *Liberating*, op. cit., 138.

pg. 73: *Patterson:* Ben Patterson, *Waiting* (Downers Grove, Ill.: InterVarsity, 1989), 109.

Unanswered Prayer: Living With the Mystery

Epigraph: George Herbert, "Deniall," *Poems*, op. cit., 96.

pg. 76: *"You have covered":* Lamentations 3:44.

pg. 77: *"Thorn":* 2 Corinthians 12:7.

pg. 77: *"Therefore I will boast":* 2 Corinthians 12:9 – 10.

pg. 77: *"Let this cup pass":* Matthew 26:39 KJV.

pg. 77: *"My God":* Matthew 27:46.

pg. 77: *"The human situation":* C. S. Lewis, *Malcolm*, op. cit., 64.

pg. 77: *"The essence of request":* C. S. Lewis, *World's*, op. cit., 4 – 5.

pg. 78: *"I tell you the truth":* Matthew 21:21.

pg. 78: *"Again, I tell you":* Matthew 18:19.

pg. 78: *"Therefore I tell you":* Mark 11:24.

pg. 78: *"You may ask":* John 14:14.

pg. 79: *"Everything that I learned":* John 15:15.

pg. 79: *"Whatever you ask":* John 14:13.

pg. 79: *"If you remain":* John 15:7.

pg. 80: *Lewis:* Lewis details this quest in the essay "Petitionary Prayer: A Problem Without an Answer," in Lewis, *Christian Reflections* (Grand Rapids, Mich.: Eerdmans, 1967), 142 – 151.

pg. 81: *"The Lord is good":* Lamentations 3:25 KJV.

pg. 81: *"But they that wait":* Isaiah 40:31 KJV.

pg. 81: *"And let us not be weary":* Galatians 6:9 KJV.

pg. 81: *"My time":* John 2:4.

pg. 82: *"Commended for their faith":* Hebrews 11:39.

pg. 82: *"God had planned":* Hebrews 11:40.

pg. 82: *"They will say":* 2 Peter 3:4, 8.

pg. 83: *Aikman:* David Aikman, *Jesus in Beijing* (Washington, D.C.: Regnery, 2003).

pg. 84: *Baillie:* John Baillie, quoted in George Appleton, *Journey for a Soul* (Glasgow: William Collins, 1974), 222.

pg. 84: *Beatitudes:* Matthew 5:3 – 11.

pg. 84: *Prayers of the Martyrs:* Duane W. H. Arnold, ed., *Prayers of the Martyrs* (Grand Rapids, Mich.: Zondervan, 1991).

pg. 85: *Goetz:* Ronald Goetz, "Lord, Teach Us to Pray," in *The Christian Century* (November 5, 1986), 975.

pg. 85: *"Salvation from our enemies"*: Luke 1:71.

pg. 87: *Rolheiser:* Richard Rolheiser, *The Holy Longing* (New York: Doubleday, 1999), 81.

pg. 88: *"I have great sorrow"*: All quotes from Paul are from Romans 9 to 11.

pg. 89: *Calvin:* John Calvin, *Sermons on the Epistle to the Ephesians* (Edinburgh, Scotland: Banner of Truth Trust, 1975), 683.

pg. 90: (footnote) *Coffin:* William Sloane Coffin, *Credo* (Louisville: Westminster/ John Knox, 2004), 40.

pg. 90: *"For my thoughts"*: Isaiah 55:8 – 9.

pg. 92: *"For now we see"*: 1 Corinthians 13:12 KJV.

What to Pray For

Epigraph: Thomas Merton, *Contemplative Prayer* (New York: Doubleday, 1996), 37.

pg. 94: *"Do you want"*: John 5:6.

pg. 94: *"Lord, the one"*: John 11:3.

pg. 94: *"Lord, if you had"*: John 11:21.

pg. 95: *"Lord, if you had"*: John 11:32.

pg. 95: *"He was deeply"*: John 11:33.

pg. 95: *"Jesus wept"*: John 11:35.

pg. 95: *Peterson:* Eugene Peterson, *Christ Plays in Ten Thousand Places* (Grand Rapids, Mich.: Eerdmans, 2005), 138.

pg. 96: *Dobson:* Ed Dobson, "Leave Room for God," in *Leadership* (Fall 2001), 31.

pg. 96: *"But if anybody"*: 1 John 2:1.

pg. 96: *Jaime Cardinal Sin:* From a private conversation with Leighton Ford and others.

pg. 97: *Lawrence:* Roy Lawrence, *How,* op. cit., 69 – 70.

pg. 97: *"Come to me"*: Matthew 11:28

pg. 98: *"Peace I leave"*: John 14:27.

pg. 98: *"In the same way"*: Romans 8:26.

pg. 100: *"So that we can"*: 2 Corinthians 1:4.

pg. 102: *A grateful heart:* From Robert A. Emmons, "Gratitude and Mind-Body Health," *Spirituality & Medicine Connection*, vol. 5, issue 1 (Spring, 2001), 1.

pg. 103: *Schmidt:* Stephen A. Schmidt, "Theologies of Prayer: A Christian Perspective," *Stauros Notebook*, vol. 20, no. 2 (September 2001), 3.

pg. 104: *"Afflicted but not crushed"*: 2 Corinthians 4:8.

pg. 104: *"As the gentle rain"*: William Shakespeare, *The Merchant of Venice*, Act 4.1, line 183.

pg. 104: *Chen:* George Chen, cited in "China's Dynamic Church," *Christianity Today* (July 13, 1998), cover story, accessed online.

pg. 105: *Van Ham:* Lee Van Ham, "Some Benefits of Losing Heart," *Faith at Work* (Spring 1998), 6 – 7.

pg. 106: *O'Connor:* Flannery O'Connor, *The Habit of Being* (New York: Vintage, 1979), 163.

pg. 107: *Roman Missal:* Aitken, *Prayers,* op. cit., 68.

pg. 107: *"Eternal glory"*: 2 Corinthians 4:17.

pg. 107: *"Christ will be"*: Philippians 1:20.

pg. 107: *"Do not worry"*: Matthew 6:25.